SEX
SE
sex
Sex
SEX
EX
SEX
S
SEX
SEX
SEX
xxx
SEX
SEX
ex
SEX
sex
EX
SEX

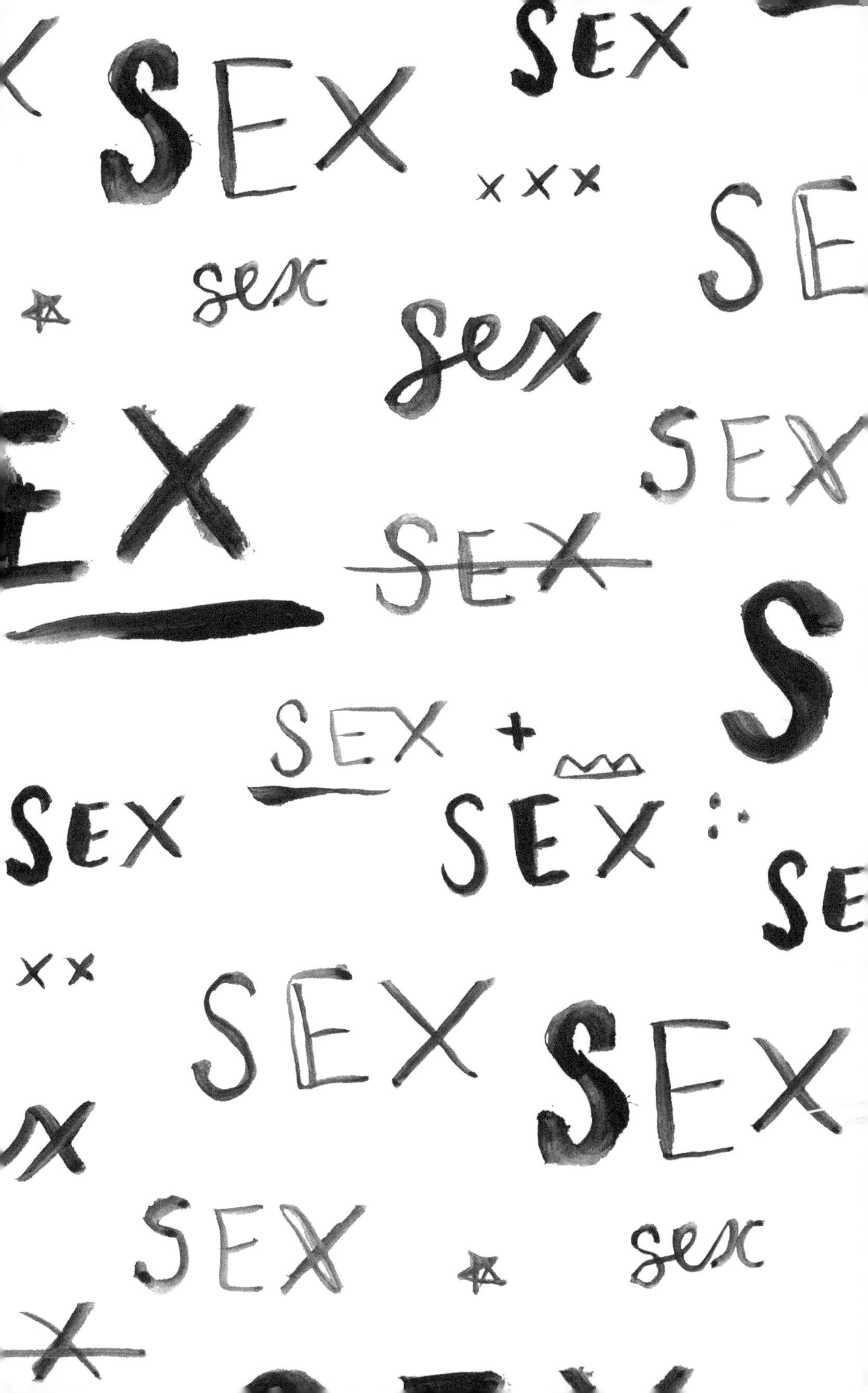
SEX
SEX
xxx
sex
sex
SEX
SEX
SEX +
SEX
SEX
xx
SEX
SEX
SEX
sex

ON TOP

The Message (MSG)
Copyright © 1993, 1994, 1995, 1996, 2000, 2001, 2002 by Eugene H. Peterson
New International Version (NIV)
Holy Bible, New International Version®, NIV® Copyright © 1973, 1978, 1984, 2011 by Biblica, Inc.®
Used by permission
All rights reserved worldwide

Design: Renae Bartley
Editor: Ruth Athanasio
Photography: Lachlan Tompsett and Elaine Kwok, Bella Thomas (headshots of Cheryl), Rachela Nardella (Pg. 111), Emma Mead (Pg. 83)
Art: Emily Averill (Chapter Art for week 1,2,3), Bel Pangburn (week 4)
Special Thanks: Karalee Fielding, Mina Kitsos, Tim Swan

DEDICATED TO,
THOSE BRAVE ENOUGH TO HAVE CONVERSATIONS
AND ASK QUESTIONS ABOUT THEIR SEXUALITY.

TAB[E OF

10
INTRO
HELLO FROM CHERYL.

14
HOW TO
READ THIS BOOK.

16
SEX GOD
WHAT GOD SAYS ABOUT SEX
(AND) SEXUALITY 101.

34
MIND
HOW SEX AFFECTS THE
ADOLOSCENT BRAIN.

46
BODY
BODY IMAGE,
GENDER IDENTITY,
HEALTH,
REPRODUCTION,
SEXUALIZATION.

66
HEART
EMOTIONS, INTIMACY, DESIRE,
SENSUALITY.

82
SOUL
HONORING GOD
AND UNDERSTANDING
YOUR VALUES.

THE STUDY

CONTENTS

103

SEX TIPS
EXPECTATIONS, BOUNDARIES, SAFER SEX.

113

REAL TALK
INTERVIEWS + REAL-LIFE STORIES.

129

BLURRED LINES
MASTURBATION, ORAL, PORN, ETC.

FOREWORD

Laura Toggs
HILLSONG YOUNG + FREE

What is it about sex?
Is it the mystery of the unknown that sparks our curiosity for those of us who have yet to have had it? Is it a misunderstanding or the miseducation of what it is intended and purposed to be for in our lives? Is it the crazed obsession that consumes our culture and media, uninvitedly bombarding us on an ever daily basis? Is it that our personal experience and the world's hype of it all doesn't line up, leaving us in an utter state of confusion or dissatisfaction? Is it that our vulnerability and fragility is either humanly protected or at threat? Is it that our value and worth is purposefully esteemed or left broken? And, is it that our identity and beliefs are in a state of emergency being challenged by an ever progressive society?
Well, could it be that it's all of this... and so much more? As young men and women - the wonderings of our soul's completion can have us trying to find the answers within our sexuality... But will we ever find it? The never ending quest to understand our sexuality is only found in understanding that its purpose was for intimate pleasure within the safety and protection of a lifetime commitment to one. But confusion enters at the point of our flawed nature as a humanity. Cheryl is a good and trusted friend of mine, passionate about her cause and intentional about educating herself and others in order to bring wholeness to as many people as possible. Our sexual choices and revelations are so important - and choosing to pick up this book to gain better understanding is the start of a pathway that leads to freedom.

+ HEY!

He was three years older (scandalous, I know!)...

On the senior rugby team at school and smelt heavily of Lynx Africa. I shut my eyes, trying not to vomit up my 14-year-old heart onto his family's lounge room floor as his tongue maneuvered its way around the inside of my mouth. He seemed to know what he was doing. Me, not so much.

Yep, that was my first kiss. And my first real encounter with physical intimacy. I was in love. I had found my soul mate. Or, so I thought. Gross, I know. But it awakened a new set of feelings (I-just-want-to-make-out-with-him-all-the-time type feelings) and questions that weren't about to go away any time soon...

I was told to 'go' and 'explore sexually' by some, while others said, "Wait until you're married!" Sexual images seem to follow me everywhere, through billboards, songs on the radio, at the cinemas, in magazines. IT WAS EVERYWHERE.

Sex-Ed at school was all STI and pregnancy prevention (which is so needed), adding to the desires taking over my thoughts - what the hell was I supposed to do?

My parents didn't shy away from talking about sex with us. They were open and honest about their experiences, which was utterly horrifying. My friends' experiences (both good and WHAT-THE-HELL stories) that emerged from weekend parties, actually got me thinking... I mean Sex-Ed ensured I knew how those bits worked, why condoms are a thing and that babies are expensive. But... How about knowing when you're ready? Surely sex can NOT just be about making babies - right? And if it's so natural, why does everyone cringe when it comes to discussion? What made it "good", or "bad"? Why does it make people more in love, or tear people apart? And why did Beyoncé make a whole album about it? #Surfboard

Allow me to introduce myself. I'm originally from California and recently married a guy name Sam - we now live in Sydney, Australia. He's a youth pastor who has devoted his life to loving and helping others. My favourite thing about him is that he keeps life simple. It's not about him, but loving and showing people Jesus. He's all-good with me being into sex; studying and talking about it...24/7. Dinner table conversations usually consist of soccer, NBA highlights, hi and low's of the day and whether masturbation is good for you or not.

I've always been really comfortable talking about sex and asking questions. As a teenager, instead of going with the flow when it came to my sexuality, I did a lot of thinking. Thinking turned into questions, which turned into research - all the while my passion started to stir. I wanted to talk, discuss and share what I had learned with others.

I wanted to tell people the truth and help each person make the best decision for themselves. As a young person, it seemed as though all the books I read hid facts in an attempt to persuade me into not having sex before marriage. My friends' sex lives didn't seem all that appealing either - so the tensions of wanting to do it, but being unsure with who, when and how had me confused.

My fascination with sex, turned into seven years of leading small discussion groups with teenage girls on sex and relationships, some regrettable exploration (ha)... studying psychology and sexology and interviews with sexologists, sex therapists and nurses... getting way too many details from my parents and friends of their experiences... short courses on sexual pleasure, courses on sexual health (like STI's and HIV), LGTBQ (Lesbian, Gay, Transgender, Bisexual and Queer) courses and way too many all-nighters reading blog after blog to understand where our culture is at when it comes to this topic. I looked at heartbreaking stats on young girls who were unhappy with their image, read way too many cheesy abstinent-only books – all while I interned at a sex clinic. You get the point - I craved information!

It's so important to know that sex is a natural and normal part of who we are even if we're not doing it! It's not shameful and dirty until you sign that wedding certificate. Sex is good, period. But don't all good things require intention?

It's essential that we start having conversations about the emotional and psychological effects it is having on young people. My aim is to bring a holistic understanding that connects the information we are traditionally given with insight on what we are not. Through analyzing the findings of neuroscientists, sexologists, brain development experts and nurses specializing in sexual health, this study is designed to equip and empower you with the knowledge and confidence to approach sex in a multi-faceted, healthy and value-driven way.

On Top is a tool to help each individual understand sexuality and enable you, the reader, to make wise choices. This study isn't meant to tell how you are supposed to live out this part of your life but it does unpack the questions that a lot of young people are asking...

+ HOW TO READ THIS BOOK

Before we dig in, here are some ground rules to get the most out of this book:

1. Put on your Sex-Positive Sunnies and embrace your sexuality as a natural and normal part of who you are.
2. Answer the questions honestly; don't just say what you think you should say.
3. Confidentiality. If you're doing this with a group, keep all information that is shared to yourself.

You can do this study either in a group or as an individual. With your group, choose one person to lead discussions - someone you trust - a friend or a youth leader. Have a quick discussion about the lens that you are reading this through. There are basically three ways individuals and societies view sex:

SEXUAL REALISM:
Which means sex is a natural appetite (like eating), nothing special about it.

SEXUAL PLATONISM:
Sex is animalistic, it's dirty and we should ONLY do it for reproduction purposes. Meaning, you should be ashamed if you enjoy it.

SEXUAL ROMANTICISM
Sex is repressed creativity and that it's actually a form of self-expression and a way to find yourself.

And then there is the **Christian view** which is that sex is sacred for three reasons; **sex procreates, sex delights and sex unifies.**

WHAT IS YOUR WORLDVIEW OF SEX?

I take my cues from the Bible, because my faith and morals shape the way I view sex.
And I believe **the Bible is sex-positive.**

1

**WHAT GOD SAYS ABOUT
SEX (AND) SEXUALITY 101**

All right guys, in this section we're going to explore what sex is and what God says about sex in the Bible. Maybe reading the word SEX makes you feel awkward or confused, curious or excited. You're not alone, it's pretty complex and there is always something new to learn about it. Often when people hear the word sex or sexuality, they think sexual intercourse. But sex is way more than just intercourse; sex is only one part of our very broad human sexuality, it has to do with our emotions, gender, reproduction, and so much more. Before we define sexuality in the next two activities, let's make sure we're all on the same page with what sex actually is. Sex isn't just physical (more than just skin on skin and fun), sex is a very broad term, and guess what, it's not just P to V. Sex is basically any activity with another person that involves the penis, vagina or bum!

Basically, sex is…

+ Sexual intercourse - penetration to vagina or bum with penis or sex toy.
+ Oral sex - mouth to genitals.
+ Some consider fingering, masturbation, mutual masturbation to be sex too.

Many people wonder what is considered "going all the way" and if it's just intercourse. All sex, even oral and anal is 'real sex', so we can say that any ***sexual behaviours that result in arousal, stimulation and gratification can be defined as sex.***

ACTIVITY

+ 5 CIRCLES

Human sexuality breaks down into five different components: everything related to human sexuality will fit in one of these circles.

List behaviours that you think fit into each circle.

INTIMACY
The ability and need to experience emotional closeness to another human and have it returned.

SENSUALITY
Awareness, acceptance of and comfort with one's own body; physiological enjoyment of one's own body and the bodies of others.

IDENTITY
The development of a sense of who one is sexually, including a sense of maleness and femaleness.

HEALTH & REPRO.
Attitudes and behaviors related to producing children, care and maintenance of the sex and reproductive organs, and health consequences of sexual behavior.

SEXUALISATION
The use of sexuality to influence, control or manipulate others.

_ DISCUSSION QUESTIONS

1. Which of the five sexuality circles feels most familiar? Least familiar? Why do you think that is so?

2. Is there any part of these five circles that you hadn't thought of as sexual before? Please explain.

3. Which circle is most important for teens to know about? Least important? Why?

4. Which circle would you be interested in discussing with your parent(s)?

5. Which circle would you be interested in talking about with someone you are dating?

+ WHAT IS SEXUALITY?

There aren't any wrong or right answers, we just want to explore. For each of the sections below, list what you have seen or heard about sex, and how these things have made you feel.

PARENTS	FRIENDS	MEDIA
Wait until you're married…	Everyone's doing it…	You'll be attractive if you wear this / buy this etc…

_ DISCUSSION QUESTIONS

1. How are the messages from parents, friends and the media similar? Different? Why do you think that is so?

2. Which messages do you agree with? Disagree with?

3. Can you think of any sexuality messages you have heard from other sources, such as religious teaching, romantic partners or health teachers?

4. If you were a parent, what is the most important sexuality message you would give your child?

5. Which of these messages could make a person feel uncomfortable with talking about sexuality?

6. Are there messages you think are incorrect and that you want more information about?

+ GOD'S INTENTION FOR HUMAN SEXUAL EXPRESSION

" TO HEAR MANY RELIGIOUS PEOPLE TALK, ONE WOULD THINK, GOD CREATED THE TORSO, HEAD, LEGS, ARMS, BUT THE DEVIL SLAPPED ON THE GENITALS."

— Don Schrader, Forbidden Fruit

Christianity doesn't say sex is bad. It says the opposite.

I don't know about you, but growing up it seemed as if the church's view on sex was a 'How-to-battle-lust' manual, with messages that sex is only good in marriage - boring! What does God actually say about sex in general?

I've found from my own experience and stories from all sorts of people that in the last few decades, sex has been a closed conversation or a taboo topic in a lot of churches. As children we are told not to have sex until we are married, but church leaders don't always talk about the why. With only the physical aspect of sexuality being overrepresented in the media and the church not addressing the topic, we have a bunch of really confused young people, often full of shame and in need of answers. It can't be ignored. Sex is a thing— prevalent in society. It's not a question about whether sex is good or bad, but what is a healthy sexuality?

God created sex and He says it is good[1]; therefore it's necessary for the Christian perspective to have a positive voice. God created sex and wants us to enjoy it.

Wait, what?

Yep, check out what Christian Sexologist (yes that's a thing) Patricia Weerakoon says, "He built us with bodies that were made for it and brains wired for sexual desire and sexual pleasure."[2] Clearly, He wants us to enjoy it, but there are boundaries with sexuality. God has a purpose for sex, and he gives us a choice (just like He doesn't make us follow Him): we can either follow His way or do our own thing.

1 Corinthians 10:23-24 says, "Looking at it one way, you could say, "Anything goes. Because of God's immense generosity and grace, we don't have to dissect and scrutinize every action to see if it will pass muster." But the point is not to just get by. We want to live well, but our foremost efforts should be to help others live well." (MSG).

THINK ABOUT WHERE YOU STAND. YOU HOLD THE AUTHORITY OVER YOUR SEXUALITY. HOW DO YOU WANT TO LIVE THIS PART OF YOUR LIFE OUT?

God says sex is sacred and throughout the Bible, we see that His plan for sex is within marriage. Pastor, theologian and Christian apologist, Tim Keller explains that sex is sacred for three different reasons; sex procreates, sex delights and sex unifies[3].

It is my belief that some of the purposes of marriage (amongst many other things) are to inspire happiness, the ability to procreate and to be intimate. Marriage is the greatest commitment we can make with another person and is actually an example of the divine union between God and humanity[4]. Sex is a gift and carries responsibility.

Consider reading the references below for examples of marriages in the Bible:

People can be madly in love, Esther and Xerxes- Esther 2:17-18
Sexual pleasure is positive, Bride and groom - Song of Songs
You'll go through tough times, Abraham and Sarah- Genesis 16-17
God will use husband and wife together, Priscilla and Aquila -1 Corinthians 16:19
Husbands and wives are to honour each other and are equal - 1 Peter 3:7 MSG
Ephesians 5:22-33 is an overall explanation of the purposes of marriage - check it out.

+ POWER COUPLE

(paraphrased by me, can be looked up in Genesis)
All right, so the first man ever, Adsy, is just chilling
in this luscious garden called Eden. It's sunny, there's
a light breeze, and he's naming animals and plants
(Scripture actually tells us God gave man - men and
women - the authority over animals, birds, and the
earth itself – whoa! okay that's intense). So he is
super busy and then God was like wait, he needs
a companion (right? Who's Jay without Beyoncé,
Kanye without Kim, Brad without Angelina, Obama
without Michelle, David Beckham without Victoria)?
Adsy takes a deeeeeep sleep, and God created a
woman out of his rib (wth? Yeah we're all thinking
it). Adsy wakes up and is like "DAMN girl!" (crucial
info about how they will become one flesh – we'll
talk about this later). For now, the important thing is
that the chapter finishes with…

They were naked and felt no shame.

+ *Relationships are a great part of life's pleasures (a gift) and they also come with great responsibility...*

GIFT

greater intimacy between two people

oneness

THE MAN SAID,

"FINALLY!

BONE OF MY BONE,
FLESH OF MY FLESH!

communication of two people

NAME HER

WOMAN

FOR SHE WAS MADE FROM

self-giving

MAN."

THEREFORE A MAN LEAVES HIS
FATHER AND MOTHER AND
EMBRACES HIS WIFE.
THEY BECOME ONE FLESH. THE TWO OF THEM,
THE MAN AND HIS WIFE, WERE NAKED,
BUT THEY FELT NO SHAME.

GENESIS 2:23-25 (MSG)

vulnerability

RESPONSIBILITY

GOD BLESSED THEM AND SAID TO THEM,
"BE FRUITFUL AND INCREASE IN NUMBER; FILL THE EARTH
AND SUBDUE IT. RULE OVER THE FISH IN THE SEA AND THE
BIRDS IN THE SKY AND OVER EVERY LIVING
CREATURE THAT MOVES ON THE GROUND."

GENESIS 1:28 (NIV)

TO BE FRUITFUL IS TO PRODUCE. GOD WANTS US TO
INCREASE IN NUMBER AND WE
REPRODUCE BY SEXUAL INTERCOURSE.
GOD COULD HAVE MADE PROCREATION SUPER
BORING AND SEND IN A FORM FOR A BABY, BUT
INSTEAD GOD GAVE US A FUN ACTIVITY.

"Sex isn't dirty...

...and it is okay to talk about."

+ OH YEAAHHH...

...check this verse out. Proverbs 5:17-20 MSG:

Your spring water is for you and you only, not to be passed around among strangers. Bless your fresh-flowing fountain! Enjoy the wife you married as a young man! Lovely as an angel, beautiful as a rose— don't ever quit taking delight in her body. Never take her love for granted! Why would you trade enduring intimacies for cheap thrills with a whore? For dalliance with a promiscuous stranger?

Obviously, God wouldn't create something for us if it wasn't good. Check out 1 Corinthians 7:1-7,

[1] Now, getting down to the questions you asked in your letter to me, First, Is it a good thing to have sexual relations? Certainly—but only within a certain context. It's good for a man to have a wife, and for a woman to have a husband. Sexual drives are strong, but marriage is strong enough to contain them and provide for a balanced and fulfilling sexual life in a world of sexual disorder. The marriage bed must be a place of mutuality—the husband seeking to satisfy his wife, the wife seeking to satisfy her husband. Marriage is not a place to "stand up for your rights." Marriage is a decision to serve the other, whether in bed or out. Abstaining from sex is permissible for a period of time if you both agree to it, and if it's for the purposes of prayer and fasting—but only for such times. Then come back together again. Satan has an ingenious way of tempting us when we least expect it. I'm not, understand, commanding these periods of abstinence—only providing my best counsel if you should choose them.

1. What is simpler about the single life?

2. Underline the two gifts God gives in this verse.

3. Does your culture honor singleness like the Bible does?

> [7] *Sometimes I wish everyone were single like me—a simpler life in many ways! But celibacy is not for everyone any more than marriage is. God gives the gift of the single life to some, the gift of the married life to others.*

1. According to this verse, what is the context that Paul is referring to?

2. In what ways can sexual drives be strong?

3. How can marriage provide a fulfilling sex life?

4. Why do you think the Bible would tell married couples not to abstain from sex for a long period of time?

5. In view of the beginning of this section, how do the purposes of sex and this passage relate?

2

**HOW SEX AFFECTS THE
ADOLESCENT BRAIN**

Do you know what your biggest sex organ is? I know what you're all thinking! No, its not below your waist... its your **brain**.

What? Yeah I know – pretty crazy!

Neuroscience (the study of the brain) shows a connection between the mind and sex.

It's important to know the science of how our brains work so that we can make choices based on both knowledge and values.

The chemicals in your brain are value-neutral. This means there is no distinction between 'good' and 'bad'. That's why it's important to know what you value so that YOU are making the decisions, not your hormones.

Bio Chemistry Love

We have three emotion systems; sex drive, attraction, and attachment. And they all are interlinked, regularly acting together, but they can also act independently (which can cause some issues in relationships). The pre-frontal cortex controls the three and we can learn to manage them[5]. We will have some fun talking about LOVE later...

" Your thoughts determine your feelings; your feelings determine your actions.

Change your thoughts, change your life."

+ RELEASES SEX HORMONES

**+ CONTROLS SEXUAL
RESPONSE: AROUSAL**

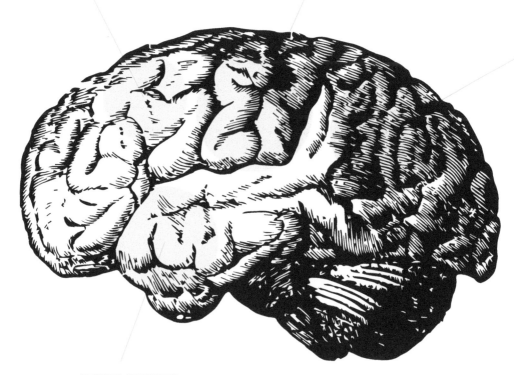

**+ SEXUAL IDENTITY:
MALE OR FEMALE**

**SEXUAL DESIRES/
FANTASIES: IMAGES
PLAYING IN YOUR MIND**

+ DEFINITIONS TO KNOW

ADOLESCENCE
(Of a young person) in the process of developing
from a child into an adult. Ages 13-26.

TO KNOW
The pre-frontal cortex is not fully developed
- this is where we make decisions and judgment calls.

VALUE NEUTRAL
Not pre-supposing the acceptance
of any particular values.

HORMONES
Major communication between different organs and
tissues. The brain is a target for many hormones.

DOPAMINE
Reward hormone: Emotional response, ability to
experience pleasure and pain.

OXYTOCIN
Pair bonding CUDDLE HORMONE
This is released during breast-feeding,
giving birth, and sexual climax.

VASOPRESSIN
Released after sex, helps strengthen commitment.
Still a lot of research to be done.

VALUES
Something we think is important, worthy, useful.

NEURONS
(In hypothalamus) release these hormones:
dopamine, oxytocin, and vasopressin.

Research shows that as an adolescent, your brain undergoes dramatic changes. These changes are not just genetic, but are greatly influenced by what is happening around you. Your environment and experiences shape your ability to make healthy judgments[6]. Dopamine is a 'pleasure' chemical that is released and processed during certain activities and plays a part in your decision making, whether you realise it or not.

_DISCUSSION QUESTIONS

1. How do you think your experiences (conversations, activities) with your friends, family, other youth are shaping your thoughts about your sex life or future sex life?

2. Do you think that your current environments like your home life, sport teams, youth ministry or school life are influencing your thoughts about yourself and sexuality?

Here is an example of dopamine at work

Say you get an A on a paper, or you received a pair of Nikes from your mum because you did chores. Dopamine is released in your brain (that 'feel good' hormone). You make a mental note to keep doing those things to achieve this 'high' again — you keep studying to receive that A again, and do more chores for mum. Dopamine works the same way in a sexual relationship. Sex in most (consensual) relationships is fun, feels good physically and creates an emotional attachment (or bond)[1] . That is, Oxytocin is released in females and Vasopressin in males. Oxytocin then causes Dopamine to be released. Since both these chemicals are value-neutral, they continue to send messages to your brain to keep repeating that activity simply because it feels good[2].

Because the adolescent brain isn't fully developed yet (the decision making skills area), it's hard to see whether the sexual relationship is having a positive or negative impact on all areas of your life[3].

The drive for sex can be very strong and as a teenager, doing it can easily become more important than things like study. Or maybe the other parts of the relationship aren't great, but you keep doing it to make your partner happy or to fit in.

On the flip side, these same chemicals can help to protect a healthy relationship and strengthen the emotional bond between two people. Oxytocin creates a unique bond between two people and connects you to your partner[4].

We're easily persuaded to to make choices based on our feelings (because of what's happening in our mind) processing all details of situation - weighing up your options, knowing your choices, deciding and then evaluating. In the next activity, we'll work out the 101 on decision making!

The brain, hormones and values are interrelated, and they influence sexual arousal. We will explore the sexual response cycle in the Body section.

ACTIVITY

+ THREE C'S TO GOOD DECISION-MAKING

1. List a challenge and answer the following questions:

2. Choices you have:

   CHOICE 1:

   CHOICE 2:

   CHOICE 3:

3. Consequences of each choice:

POSTITIVE	NEGATIVE

   Your decision is:

   Your reason is:

_ DISCUSSION QUESTIONS

1. Would certain consequences warn you right away to choose something else? If so what are they? (e.g. a risk to your health or someone else's; a risk of losing integrity?)

2. What negative consequences relate to a person's feelings or values (e.g. guilt about choosing against values; feeling bad for doing something your parents, church, or friends would disapprove of; feeling used or exploited.)

3. When facing a challenge, how could you find other choices? (e.g. talk to youth leader, parent, school counselor or other trusted adult.)

4. How can you explore all the possible consequences of a particular choice? Who can you talk to and how can they help?

5. Are you facing a decision now? Could you use this model to help you?

BODY

3

**BODY IMAGE
GENDER IDENTITY
HEALTH
REPRODUCTION
SEXUALIZATION**

+ BODY IMAGE

Awareness and acceptance of one's own body

There are countless studies showing how young people are not happy with their bodies. Research from the U.S. Department of Health and Human Services shows that body image and self-esteem go hand-in-hand — young people with poor self image tend to get involved in 'harmful' situations, i.e. substance abuse, unsafe friendships, rushing into sex, self harm[1].

The media tells us how our bodies should look. Unfortunately, the message it gives is an unrealistic standard for both boys and girls to act and behave in a certain way.

" NOW EVERY GIRL IS EXPECTED TO HAVE CAUCASIAN BLUE EYES, FULL SPANISH LIPS, A CLASSIC BUTTON NOSE, HAIRLESS ASIAN SKIN WITH A CALIFORNIA TAN, A JAMAICAN DANCE HALL ASS, LONG SWEDISH LEGS, SMALL JAPANESE FEET, THE ABS OF A LESBIAN GYM OWNER, THE HIPS OF A NINE-YEAR-OLD BOY, THE ARMS OF MICHELLE OBAMA, AND DOLL TITS."

— Tina Fey

Do you ever wonder why the media has such influence and impact on the way we view ourselves? The media is clever; instead of speaking to our intellect, they speak to our emotions[2]. By speaking into people's desires and using fear–tactics, they have the power to make us believe we need a particular product to be accepted, pretty, valuable, cool, etc.

We compare ourselves to everyone around us and with people in the media. This has lead us to criticise ourselves and focus on what we're 'lacking' - no wonder depression rates are so high! Comparison is the thief of joy but the key to overcoming it is gratitude and being grateful for what we do have.

There is hope! The Bible actually talks about our image. This foundational truth can shape the way we view ourselves.

Genesis 1:26-27 God spoke: "Let us make human beings in our image, make them reflecting our nature"… "God created human beings; he created them godlike, reflecting God's nature. He created them male and female."

Do you get what this actually means? The Creator of the earth made you and me like Him! The amazing attributes of a man are actually a direct reflection of God and the attributes of a woman reflect another side of Him, which is why we are equal. Like God, you are creative, you are intelligent, you are spiritual, you are a communicator, you have a sense of morality and you have a purpose.

I realise this can sound cliché or a bit cheesy, but it's a truth in the Bible that is so often misunderstood. Psalm 139:13-16 (MSG) says, "Oh yes, you shaped me first inside, then out; you formed me in my mother's womb. I thank you, High God—you're breathtaking! Body and soul, I am marvelously made! I worship in adoration—what a creation! You know me inside and out, you know every bone in my body; You know exactly how I was made, bit by bit, how I was sculpted from nothing into something. Like an open book, you watched me grow from conception to birth; all the stages of my life were spread out before you. The days of my life all prepared before I'd even lived one day."

It's my belief that our life stories don't start at conception. Life begins before our parents even met. God knew you. He knew you then and He knows you now. He cares about you, He loves you regardless of your upbringing or the choices you've made. He has a plan just for you.

+ DEFINITIONS TO KNOW

BIOLOGICAL SEX
Determined by chromosomes (XX girl or XY boy), internal and external anatomies. People with chromosomes different from XX or XY are called intersex.

GENDER
Societal and cultural norms of what it means to be male or female.
Gender identity and expression is a person's perception of themselves as either male or female, and how they express themselves as a boy or girl.

GENDER ROLES
Some depend on the way male/female bodies are built - females menstruate, males produce sperm. Some roles are placed by specific cultures on how people should act, think and feel based on biological sex. Placed by specific cultures of how people should act, think, feel based on biological sex.

SEXUAL ORIENTATION
Sexual orientation is the sexual attraction of an individual to others of opposite, same or both sexes.

+ LOVERS

There is no room for homophobia – how Christians can support the LGBTQ community.

The main thing about being a Christian is to love. Jesus greatest commandment is to love - God first and then others.

We're called to be lovers of ALL people—not to judge them. I have a strong conviction that God does not see us by our sexual orientation or gender.

He simply loves us just for ourselves - we can't earn His love or do anything to push His love away.

The journey for young people figuring out their sexuality isn't easy. There is so much pressure from home, the media, bullying at school.

Put yourself in their shoes, their inner-thoughts and the confusion they could be going through.

Labels aren't for people.

The inclusive nature of the Gospel shows us that we shouldn't exclude people based on their gender identity or sexual orientation.

Jesus loved and accepted all different types of people[2].

Tim Keller puts it this way, "Tolerance is not about not having beliefs, it's about how do we treat people that don't agree with what we believe".

Jesus was the ultimate homie – He was friends with everyone[3].

+ IT'S A GIRL / BOY THING

Recognizing stereotypes

Although we can easily laugh at some of these, the truth is, stereotypes are made-up pressures and expectations that society and culture place on both sexes and they can be harmful. These stereotypes imply that if you're a boy that doesn't fit the "masculine" criteria, or a girl that doesn't fit the "feminine" criteria, something is wrong with you.

THIS IS A LIE. It's okay for boys to cry and wear pink. It's okay for girls to hate make-up and drive sports cars. These things don't make you any less of a man or woman. It's perfectly normal.

SHEESH. Can't we all just relax and embrace each other?!

BOYS
TO BE MASCULINE

Man up/ roar
Boys don't cry
Guys have to initiate sex or relationships, big trucks, no emotions, be in control, take risks to prove manhood, money = status, be sexually active - oh and with lots of partners, be the 'breadwinner', violent

GIRLS
TO BE FEMININE

"You run like a girl"
Gossip, go to the gym, emotional, dependent on a man, shopping, uptight, dramatic, need a man to do basic things, have to be sexual to be attractive, assume responsibility for rape, take careers in "helping" professions

_ DISCUSSION QUESTIONS

1. What are societies' pressures on gender?

2. How can we be the change?

Sexual Response Cycle

Masters and Johnson (1966) defined the sexual response cycle into four phases. Other theories have been researched since then, but this study is one that has shown to be consistent. It is a generalisation because it's based on just the physical aspects such as culture and relationship status, however, other impacting factors were not taken into consideration.

The four phases

1. EXCITEMENT: Myotonia - muscles tense, heart rate increases, flushed skin, vasocongestion - swelling of genitals (penis erection and swelling of labia). Essentially, the sexual organs are preparing for intercourse.

2. PLATEAU: An advanced stage of the excitement phase that stays constant until orgasm.

3. ORGASM: For males, it occurs in two stages of muscular contractions - release or ejaculation of semen and sensations of pleasure happen. For females, it's contractions of the pelvic muscles that surround the vagina. Orgasms are talked about as an out of this world experience! It's important to know that sexual pleasure or satisfaction aren't dependant on orgasm - they don't happen every time a person has sex.

4. RESOLUTION: The body returns to the pre-aroused state. For males, there is a refractory period, which means they cannot be stimulated sexually for a while and reach orgasm again, whereas females can.

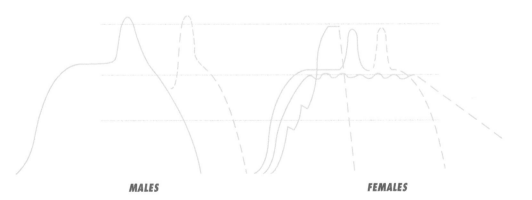

MALES   FEMALES

"Educating you empowers you healthy choice your values."

elf
o make
based on

+ HEALTH

Checklist for a sexually healthy adolescent...

☐ Accepts their own body.

☐ Communicates with family, friends, and partners.

☐ Has knowledge of facts.

☐ Understands risks and consequences of sexual activity.

☐ Knows what intercourse is.

☐ Has knowledge of human anatomy.

☐ Has the skills to set appropriate sexual boundaries.

☐ Is informed with contraception (pills, condoms, etc).

☐ Knows how to use and access health care systems.

+ *REPRODUCTION AND ANATOMY*

Reproduction: Making babies!

God tells us to be fruitful and multiply.
Some people dream of having children, while others could not
think of anything worse. Both are okay.
Some people have unexpected pregnancies, while others try for
years to fall pregnant.

For those who are having sex who aren't ready for kids,
contraception is especially important to avoid a pregnancy.

However, the only 100% effective way to not fall pregnant, is not
to have sex at all.

Sexual anatomy: Internal and external sexual organs.

The female body and male body have different anatomies —
external sex anatomies would be genitals and internal anatomies
are reproductive organs (like ovaries).

Not all female anatomies look the same, and neither do all male
anatomies, with many different sizes and colours in existence.
It's common to wonder if you look 'normal'. (The media and
porn industries in particular, give us a false standard for what our
bodies need to look like e.g. smooth, light, no hair etc.)

Overall, watching pornography has unhealthy and damaging
impacts on not only the viewers, but on our society. Porn only
shows one side of sex - the physical side, which is not actually a
realistic depiction and this shapes our expectations of sex, gender
and identity. In the magazine section, I expand on what happens
in a person's mind when they watch porn, so check that out.

SEXUAL HARASSMENT

Unwanted sexual behaviour that makes you feel uncomfortable - can be physical or verbal.

PORN

Authentic sexuality is replaced by unrealistic expectations, setting people up for a disappointing sex life.

RAPE / INCEST

35% of women worldwide have experienced sexual violence in their lifetime. One in three girls and one in six boys have been sexually abused by the time they are 16[5].

+ SEXUALIZATION

SEXTING

A product of social pressure: "Damned if you do, damned if you don't", "slut" if you do, "prude" if you don't. 88% of images sent to a person (of sender's choice) are then sent to others/put on the Internet/ uploaded to porn sites.

MEDIA

The media shapes our worldview (how we interpret reality and what we believe to be true). 'Sex sells' across film, music, food, TV; even ads for the deodorant we buy are sexualised. Sex appeal is a currency.

SEXISM

Disliking or discriminating against someone because of their gender.

DID YOU KNOW: "the odds of being attacked by a shark are 1 in 3,748,067, while a woman's odds of being raped are 1 in 6? Yet fear of sharks is seen as rational, while being cautious of men is seen as misandry (man-hating)." -- #YesAllWomen Movement

+ *HYPER-SEXUALIZED CULTURE*

[sexualize: to make things sexual (when they don't need to be) / culture: way we dress, words we use, what we value]

A hyper-sexualised culture sees excessive sexual influence and exposure as the norm.

Romans 12:2, "Do not conform to the pattern of this world, but be transformed by the renewing of your mind. Then you will be able to test and approve what God's will is — his good, pleasing and perfect will."

We've got to think back to what Paul says in Romans — he tells us "Do not conform to the pattern of this world". So where does that leave us as Christians?

Living according to the Bible is counter-cultural — it goes against society's norms. This doesn't need to be in a super obvious, 'in your face' type of way. For example, society says its dehumanizing to not indulge into ALL your sexual desires, but the Bible says it's a gift to be handled with care. This often requires sacrifice.

The whole 'not having sex' thing isn't merely about following 'rules' of Christianity. But as believers, Jesus does ask us to do life a bit differently in some areas. This 'not having sex before marriage' thing is a way to honor God with our bodies. That's why we make this sacrifice.

So, now we know the why... that brings us to the next question: How do we not conform to the culture we live in?

ACTIVITY

+ *FIGHTING INFLUENCES AND FOLLOWING THROUGH*

Use your decision from activity three.

Your decision is:

Influences that might change your mind are:

1.

2.

3.

4.

Things you can do to fight the influence are:

1.

2.

3.

4.

_DISCUSSION QUESTIONS

1. Adults often accuse teenagers of not making good decisions, but often making the decisions is the easy part. Staying with the decision can be much more difficult. Describe a situation in which you were trying to stick to a decision and other things were influencing you to change it.

2. Which influences are the most difficult for young people to resist? Why?

3. What decisions do young people often make and have trouble following through with? What usually influences them to change their decisions?

4. Who could help you follow through with an important decision?

HEART

4

**EMOTIONS
INTIMACY
DESIRE
SENSUALITY**

"ABOVE ALL ELSE, GUARD YOUR HEART, FOR EVERYTHING YOU DO FLOWS FROM IT"

— Proverbs 4:23 NIV

When it comes to our sexuality and the heart, the advice we can get from this proverb is to take it sloooow, love yourself, look out for red-flags, don't settle, talk to someone you trust about the relationship, consider timing and make choices out of critical thinking – not fuzzy feelings.

Emotions: feelings one has, deriving from circumstances, moods, and/or relationships with others[1].

"We are psychologically, emotionally, cognitively and spiritually hardwired for connection, love, and belonging", says research professor Brené Brown in her book Daring Greatly: How the Courage to Be Vulnerable Transforms the Way we Live, Love, Parent and Lead.

Love is a human necessity. Before you can love anyone else and truly feel loved, it's important that you love yourself. Some are searching for that love and acceptance (in good and bad places).

Side Note: true and genuine love is honest, non-judgmental, self-giving, and unconditional – meaning nothing is expected in return. Love is more than a feeling; it's an action.

Dr. Helen Fisher is an anthropologist and human researcher with many focuses, one being the chemistry of romantic love. Thanks to her and many other researchers, scientists and psychologists, we have a better understanding of how love works within ourselves, and the role that it plays in society. Fisher's research has enabled me to educationally form my own thoughts and opinions regarding love, which we will look over in the next section, The Force of Love.

Another little side note: God told mankind to be fruitful and multiply. He designed us with brains that seek/yearn for a partner to fulfill this commandment.

Because this study is all about understanding sexuality, we're going to look at how the need for romantic love works within us.

Let's break it down...

LOVE TAKES EFFORT

Love isn't just a feeling – it is a choice and commitment. At some point between 18 months and 3 years into a relationship, feelings of being 'love-drunk' start to fade (not LOVE, but feelings of an obsessive nature). Then the deeper level of the relationship shows – like the commitment and stability of knowing what's actually going on between the two people. (AWWWwww, cute!)

When the spark fades away, couples may think that the love was never real, or that it is over. But while those honeymoon feelings don't stay forever, true love does last! When you truly know someone on an intimate level, you learn how to keep it exciting and fresh. (*Cough* – so this is "one purpose" for sex in marriage, to give the unity strength).

Some people yearn for that love rush, which can be both self-destructive and selfish. It can work like an addiction, with a person going from relationship to relationship just for that special feeling. Heartbreakers, hey?! It actually has a term: *limerence*. Limerence occurs in the attraction stage – it's that feeling of being lovesick. The catch is, it's impossible to stay there forever and delay the relationship from developing deeper into the attachment stage.

THE FORCE OF LOVE
Sex drive - Attraction - Attachment

Essentially romantic attraction is driven by our sex drive and the 'need' for a partner; attraction helps us to stay focused on one person and attachment's purpose is to bring union between two people (and then reproduce).

Sex drive - libido: FIND ME A PARTNER/LOVER

Attraction stage: OMG I LOVE HIM(OR HER)!! In this stage you've already done the instagram stalk, you can't muster up a sentence in front of that person, think butterflies-heart beating. Awkward encounters have been the norm. THEY TAKE OVER YOUR THOUGHTS, sort of obsessed with them - you're thinking of strategies of how you're going to get this to the next level.

Ha, okay so you get it— so in this stage if the relationship does actually start (beyond the stalking) its a lot of fun, its a special time of getting to know each other, it's very exciting, it's a novelty-the newness and freshness. Like Dr. Fisher says, you may experience separation anxiety, emotional dependence, and obsessive thinking[2].

Dopamine pushes you to fall in love with this person.

Attachment: this is where SEEEEX comes in. When you ORGASM, that releases oxytocin and vasopressin, lots and lots of it which gives you that feeling of attachment. Attachment gives us social comfort, emotional union, peace, and closeness with a long-term partner.

Some people are attracted to someone, date them, sleep together (married or not) and become attached. Sometimes people sleep together first and then fall in love. The three stages don't always work in a particular order.

There is enough research and you can probably look at the relationships around you to see that healthy relationships are founded on true/deep friendships and operate on an intimate level.

In the next activity, we will explore notions of how you give and receive love in relationships.

ACTIVITY

+ THE 5 LOVE LANGUAGES TEST

Each person gives and receives love in different ways. This test will help define that for you! It's good information to know for every relationship (parents, besties, and that special someone). Understanding yourself, better equips you to have power to make the right choices, communicate more effectively and have healthier relationships.

_ DIRECTIONS

Go to http://www.5lovelanguages.com/profile/teens/

Print and answer the questions or take the quiz online. The letter that gets the most points is your most important love language.

WHAT ARE YOUR RESULTS?

Check the highest two:

A. ____ Words of affirmation
B. ____ Quality time
C. ____ Gifts
D. ____ Acts of service
E. ____ Physical touch

WORDS OF AFFIRMATION: Encouraging words, compliments, cards/letters.

QUALITY TIME: Undivided attention, taking trips, doing things together.

GIFTS: Giving gifts, remembering special occasions.

ACTS OF SERVICE: House chores, asking "What can I do for you?".

PHYSICAL TOUCH: Hugs, pats, sitting close, facial expressions, non-verbal.

+ INTIMACY

The ability and need to experience emotional closeness to another human being and have it returned[3].

A common misconception is that intercourse is the 'be-all and end-all' of intimacy. There is a natural need for humans to have intimacy, but intimacy is not just physical. Non-sexual and non-romantic relationships can be just as intimate as sexual relationships. Sex is just one way of being intimate with someone.

We learn intimacy through our upbringing — how we relate to our parents, siblings, guardians, family and friends. Personal experiences while growing up teach us how to connect with people on different levels.

We are all raised differently – some of us were taught healthy intimate boundaries, while others were not. Everyone is raised with a different set of experiences and as a result, the boundaries of what is considered appropriate vary from person to person.

Sometimes the past can affect someone from being intimate, whether it was because of a particular life-choice they made, or something that happened to them. It's important to recognize when and where these barriers exist, and to seek the help of a trusted adult who you can talk to; someone who can help you work through it.

Healthy intimacy has boundaries and you're free to be your (true) self with another person.

When it comes to a romantic relationship, we can easily rush the process of organically getting to know someone because we're letting the physical appetite determine our choices. The need for intimacy is natural and a good thing, but that doesn't necessarily mean it needs to be expressed physically. Sometimes the friendship and depth or maturity of a relationship may not be ready for the physical stuff. You don't want that to replace truly getting to know someone.

You don't need to have sex with someone to show them that you love them. I'm saying this because people can be manipulated into having sex by their partner, asking/forcing them to 'prove' their love. If you're not into it, it's important they respect your decision and wait.

We need to make sure that we protect the ability to connect intimately with someone. Not everyone gets to be on that deep level with you.

Here are ways we can build intimacy in our relationships

Sharing feelings
Sharing fears
Talk about the future and dreams
Being honest
Letting our guard down
Being open
Trusting

When experiencing true intimacy, you'll notice feelings of acceptance – that you're accepted and valued just because of who you are; like you really know that person and that you are truly known. It's peaceful.

Another thing worth mentioning is that it can be really easy to misinterpret being "close" to someone as actually being intimate with them. Being close can lead to codependency; this is when you're in a relationship with someone and you become dependent (or even addicted) to them in an unhealthy way.

"Dependency may appear to be love because it is a force that causes people to fiercely attach themselves to one another. But in actuality it is not love; it is a form of anti love. It has its genesis in a parental failure to love and it perpetuates the failure. It seeks to receive rather than to give. It nourishes infantilism rather than growth. It works to trap and constrict rather than to liberate. Ultimately, it destroys rather than builds relationships, and it destroys rather than builds people[19]."
— M. Scott Peck

Whew, that's a bit heavy! Basically…
Being dependent on someone for a feeling of approval, belonging or love, while hiding parts of ourselves or changing ourselves, is not healthy. I'm not saying we need to be completely transparent with everyone — it is your choice who you decide to be open with. An amazing part of intimacy is that you are only intimate with particular people. Letting people into the deepest part of you can feel risky but it is a positive risk if it is with a safe person.

What Is A Safe Person?

A safe person is someone whom you trust, who has good intentions and moral characteristics. Someone who is caring, honest, and someone your family and friends approve of!

+ PLAYA PLAYA

Heard these one liners before?

Chances are they were trying to get more than you were prepared to give. These statements are red flags (to get away) - lines that people use when they are trying to get something out of you.

"IF YOU REALLY LIKED ME, YOU WOULD _____"

"WHY ARE YOU SO UP-TIGHT?" "IT'S NOT THAT BIG OF A DEAL"

"EVERYONE ELSE IS DOING IT"

"THE CONNECTION WILL FADE AWAY IF WE DON'T"

ALWAYS GOING ON ABOUT A "SPECIAL BOND", BUT NOT ACTUALLY MAKING A COMMITMENT TO YOU.

"I THOUGHT YOU WERE DIFFERENT"

"I WON'T TELL ANYONE, IT'S JUST BETWEEN US TWO"

"ITS JUST _____, NOT LIKE WE'RE GOING ALL THE WAY"

These statements often make you question yourself – "Is it that big of a deal? Oh my gosh – am I being uptight?!" They are intended to make you feel embarrassed or guilty, to prompt a certain response. Be confident with where you stand. If they don't respect you,

Give them the flick...

+ DESIRE

[dih-zahyuh r]
(n) Is a sense of longing or hoping for a person, object, or outcome[20].

Ever wonder why that whole 'friends with benefits' thing rarely works out. Remember in section one, about brain chemicals? The cuddle hormone, Oxytocin and Vasopressin are released – without you even realizing. Sexy time connects you on a deeper level – which is a good thing, right? It's what helps us stay connected to a significant other, allowing us to have a special bond with someone.

The decisions we make as an individual do affect people around us and the people in our future. As a sexually healthy adolescent, it is vital to make decisions based on the big picture (values, health and the context of a relationship), not just current feelings.

Which brings us to the topic of desire.

Desire for physical and emotional intimacy is natural; a great gift to humanity (HELLO – thank you God), but it can be tricky to navigate. Author, essayist and Christian apologist C.S. Lewis put it brilliantly: "…sex in itself is 'normal' and 'healthy'… The lie consists in the suggestion that any sexual act… is also normal or healthy".[21] Just because someone desires something doesn't always mean they should have it. However, this thought is so counter-cultural. Society tells us we can have whatever we want, however, and whenever, we want. Sexual indulgence is NOT healthy. Like the desire for sex, we also have the desire to eat. Imagine you have unlimited access to ice cream; all the flavors, all the mix-ins and toppings you want. You could have as many scoops as you like, so you just keep eating and eating and eating until you end up sick and vomiting. Yep – pretty gross. While it would be lovely to just have everything we've always wanted, life (unfortunately) doesn't work that way. We need boundaries. We need to be able to know our limits and not have an excess amount of ice cream just because we can. It's not healthy. Pressure from the media tells us it's dehumanizing to not act on our sexual desires but no one has ever died from a lack of sex.

Questions like, "Do I act on every desire I feel?" or "Can I have sex with whomever I want?" are legitimate…

MAINSTREAM: SEX ISN'T WORTH ANYTHING, WHO CARES, DO WHATEVER. REALITY: IT IS GOING TO COST YOU SOMETHING; THERE ARE CONSEQUENCES.

i.e. Sleeping with your friend's ex just because she's hot and easy or unprotected sex because it was the heat of the moment, is not a good idea. Sex in the wrong circumstances can leave you feeling broken, used, with an STI or suffering other devastating consequences.

Sometimes reality isn't pretty, but equipping yourself with the knowledge of sex will set you up for a win. Desire is good, but having healthy boundaries is the key.

+ SENSUALITY

[sen-shoo-al-i-tee]
(n) (p) Awareness, acceptance of one's own body and ability to express it
positively with one's self and with others.

Erotica in the Bible?! YES.

Did you know there is a whole book in the Bible dedicated to the passionate
love between two lovers before they marry? They are expressing the desires they
have for each other, yet are clearly waiting until they are married (as difficult as
that may sound) to act on them. It's called Song of Songs and it's a great image
of emotions, desires and sensuality between two people.

Song of Songs stands out from the Bible's other books because it is a raw,
realistic explanation of physical love within marriage.

Have you ever been in a situation where two friends are going at it; making out,
like no one is around. Maybe you've seen this around school, in a shopping
centre, and you think, "get a grip people, get a room…"

Well, the book of Song of Songs is kind of like that — we're getting a sneak peak
at the romantic love and sexual tension between a couple. How is it that most
people think God hates and shames sex?! The fact that this book is Bible-worthy
is evidence that God wants us to know SEX IS GOOD.

Why do you think God put this book in the Bible?

1:2-4 Kiss me—full on the mouth! Yes! For your love is better than wine, headier than your aromatic oils. The syllables of your name murmur like a meadow brook. No wonder everyone loves to say your name! Take me away with you! Let's run off together! An elopement with my King-Lover! We'll celebrate, we'll sing, we'll make great music. Yes! For your love is better than vintage wine. Everyone loves you—of course! And why not?

4:1-15 The Man talking

4:16 Wake up, North Wind, get moving, South Wind! Breathe on my garden, fill the air with spice fragrance. Oh, let my lover enter his garden! Yes, let him eat the fine, ripe fruits.

5:1-2 [The Man] I went to my garden, dear friend, best lover! breathed the sweet fragrance.
I ate the fruit and honey, I drank the nectar and wine. Celebrate with me, friends! Raise your glasses—"To life! To love!"
[The Woman] I was sound asleep, but in my dreams I was wide awake. Oh, listen! It's the sound of my lover knocking, calling!

They did it

7:9-13 Yes, and yours are, too—my love's kisses flow from his lips to mine. I am my lover's.
I'm all he wants. I'm all the world to him!
Come, dear lover— let's tramp through the countryside. Let's sleep at some wayside inn,
then rise early and listen to bird-song. Let's look for wildflowers in bloom, blackberry bushes blossoming white, Fruit trees festooned
with cascading flowers. And there I'll give myself to you, my love to your love!
Love-apples drench us with fragrance, fertility surrounds, suffuses us,
Fruits fresh and preserved that I've kept and saved just for you, my love.

two aren't joking tennion is hot!

8:10 Dear brothers, I'm a walled-in virgin still,
but my breasts are full— And when my lover sees me, he knows he'll soon be satisfied.

Some people have strong sexual desires and maybe you're at a stage where you don't really, but all your friends do, that's okay, we're all different. It's okay for us to have sexual desires or not too.

What have you learned about sex from Song of Songs?

"Your worth is NOT based on your sexual choices."

SOUL

5

HONORING GOD AND UNDERSTANDING YOUR VALUES

" *CAUSE TONIGHT IS THE NIGHT WHEN TWO BECOME ONE."*

— *Spice Girls (1996)*

Why 7-year-old Cheryl and countless kids around the world know all the lyrics to this particular song is a mystery to me. Still, who would have thought that the Spice Girls were basically theologians preaching from Genesis, singing "they became one flesh". This biblical concept of two becoming one through sex is something neuroscience today explains through chemical bonding.

Our soul and heart are similar; they are our very core as a human. Like we discussed in the last chapter, we need to protect our heart and be intentional about what we are feeding our soul.

"Two become one," means that two souls are coming together in the most intimate way possible - to protect and enhance the relationship between two people. This is absolutely incredible; if there was one thing I wanted someone to understand it would be that.

Get to know someone, have fun, go on dates, be intentional, focus on friendship (sex isn't everything, you will spend a lot more time talking and doing the mundane things together than having sex all the time). Build trust, don't settle, put each other first and then once you've created that healthy culture within a relationship, let the physical side of intimacy protect and grow that relationship in the right time.

To have a well-rounded understanding of sexuality we should explore science - biological and psychological, emotional, and physical studies. Sexuality is the same across the board (whether Christian or not). But, as a Christian we add morals (standards of behaviour) to that list of understanding.

(Morals differ from culture to culture, and between laws and religions. We shouldn't hold people accountable to Christian morals, unless they consider themselves a Christian i.e. don't impose your beliefs on someone else.)

The Bible tells us to "Honour God with your body". But what does that even mean?

+ HONOR

[ON-ER]
(n) What it is: High respect or doing something that is morally right
(v) How to do it: Regard with high respect, fulfill (an obligation) or keep an agreement.

HONOR IS THE COURAGE TO DO WHAT IS RIGHT.

1 Corinthians 6:16-20 tells us why we should honor God with our sexuality, check it out -

"There's more to sex than mere skin on skin. Sex is as much spiritual mystery as physical fact. As written in Scripture, "The two become one." Since we want to become spiritually one with the Master, we must not pursue the kind of sex that avoids commitment and intimacy, leaving us lonelier than ever—the kind of sex that can never "become one." There is a sense in which sexual sins are different from all others. In sexual sin we violate the sacredness of our own bodies, these bodies that were made for God-given and God-modeled love, for "becoming one" with another. Or didn't you realize that your body is a sacred place, the place of the Holy Spirit? Don't you see that you can't live however you please, squandering what God paid such a high price for? The physical part of you is not some piece of property belonging to the spiritual part of you. God owns the whole works. So let people see God in and through your body." (MSG)

So, how can we honor God with our sexuality?

Simply by honorable behaviours (e.g. honesty, integrity, respect, dignity).

Whether you are single, dating, heartbroken, in love, exploring, (and if you go to the back we have an article on dating and just being able to understand when you're ready for it), you have to have a vision for your dating life or else you'll settle. Know what you want and what you don't want, decide how you will live out your sexuality, don't let pressure from people or the need to feel accepted control this part of your life.

I know that might be easier said than done. If you're comfortable, you should talk with someone older who can help and give advice - ideally someone with the same values as you. You can also contact us at cherylfagan.org.

Living in an honorable way takes some thinking - insight into your pursuits on life.

Are you after a meaningful life or a happy life?

HAPPY LIFE – TAKER. All about the here and now, the feelings are fleeting and ultimately fade.

MEANINGFUL LIFE – GIVER. Connects past and present with the future. It endures and finds meaning in the suffering.

Our soul is who we are. The choices and behaviours we make shape who we are (and our future).
A meaningful life will be determined by the state of our soul.

It's easy to do what 'feels good' or what 'makes me happy', but doing what is right produces depth of character and life.

A successful 'self' or healthy self/soul is living by our values.

HOW DO WE LOOK AFTER OUR SOUL?

Knowing our values and exercising self-discipline is the key to not just a happy but a healthy life.

It takes courage and self-discipline to live by your values. Discipline is your friend, it is not a punishment - discipline is a teacher. The Bible goes as far as calling discipline a path to life![3] It's super important to make wise choices - it's for our own benefit[1].

Psychotherapist, Russ Harries explains, "Values are important because they can guide you and motivate you through situations where your feelings might lead you off course. Acting in accordance with your own deepest values is inherently satisfying and fulfilling – even though it often forces you to face your fears."
Fears could be rejection, loneliness or judgment.

+ *VALUES 101*

Foundation of our lives are built from them

Foundations of our romantic relationships are built from them

They justify how we live our life

They tell us what we are for and against

Know them and you'll live by them

They guide you through life

They help you make decisions

If you feel guilty about a choice you made it's that you behaved in a way that went against your values

They are shaped by our upbringing, friends, faith, etc.

Values change as we grow and mature and experience new things.

"Sex can not be used as an exchange...

(for popularity, to keep a BF / GF, love or belonging)."

ACTIVITY

+ VALUES

Why do you think knowing your values will help you make better decisions?

PART 1: VALUES AND BEHAVIOR

1. How do you know you're making your own decisions and not someone else's?

2. What happens when your values are different from your parents? We might have different values from our parents, but as a teenager, you need to respect what they ask. Do you talk to them about how you feel? Do you get angry or close up?

3. What happens when your values are different from your friends? Are you cool with that?

4. What happens when your values line up differently than church? When someone does something against church values, they can easily have feelings of guilt, anger or embarrassment; so much so that people will often leave the church. But chances are your youth leader or others around you have dealt with a similar situation and could help you walk through it. If you have a different value from church, do you feel like you would have to choose between that situation or relationship and church?

PART 2: WE LEARN VALUES FROM OUR FAMILIES AND UPBRINGING, SO LETS DO SOME REFLECTING TO UNDERSTAND HOW THEY WERE SHAPED.

	What your parent or guardian thinks	What you think?	Is it different/same and why?
Values about dating			
Values about sexuality			
Values about independence			
Values about religion			
What behaviours are not tolerated?			

What values would you want your kids to understand about the above?

Can you think of a couple who inspire you?

What qualities do they have?

PART 3: VALUES AND BEHAVIOUR

1. Circle three that you identify strongly with.

Self control, honesty, accountability, integrity, equality, openness, selflessness, obedience, inner-harmony, love, vulnerability, sacrifice, unity.

2. Do you practice these in all your relationships? (parents, friends)

3. What makes them challenging?

4. How can you make them easier to live by?

Below are statements that reflect a value. Do the behaviours listed support or ignore the value?

I value equality.
I would encourage a girl to take an advanced physics class.
I think it's okay for a girl to ask a boy out.
The guy should always pay for a date.

I value honesty.
I wouldn't share my true feelings with my bf/gf in case they broke up with me.
As long as the person is saying what I like to hear.

Having sex is a good thing.
If you are in love, it doesn't matter what age you are.
As long as you know the health risks and use protection.
When you're married.

If your values aren't lining up with your behaviour, should you reconsider your values or behaviour?

66 *WHEN YOU GO THROUGH LIFE GUIDED BY YOUR VALUES, NOT ONLY DO YOU GAIN A SENSE OF VITALITY AND JOYFULNESS, BUT YOU ALSO EXPERIENCE THAT LIFE CAN BE RICH, FULL AND MEANINGFUL, EVEN WHEN BAD THINGS HAPPEN[23]."*

— *Russ Harris*

**HOW WE LIVE OUT OUR SEXUALITY IS A RESPONSE TO HOW WE SEE GOD'S
LOVE FOR US AND WHAT HE HAS DONE FOR US.**

We shouldn't abuse (or take advantage) the free grace He gives us, e.g. sin and
pray for forgiveness later[3]

Check out Galatians 5:19-23,

*It is obvious what kind of life develops out of trying to get your own way all
the time: repetitive, loveless, cheap sex; a stinking accumulation of mental and
emotional garbage; frenzied and joyless grabs for happiness; trinket gods; magic-
show religion; paranoid loneliness; cutthroat competition; all-consuming-yet-
never-satisfied wants; a brutal temper; an impotence to love or be loved; divided
homes and divided lives; small-minded and lopsided pursuits; the vicious
habit of depersonalizing everyone into a rival; uncontrolled and uncontrollable
addictions; ugly parodies of community. I could go on.*
*This isn't the first time I have warned you, you know. If you use your freedom
this way, you will not inherit God's kingdom.*
*But what happens when we live God's way? He brings gifts into our lives, much
the same way that fruit appears in an orchard—things like affection for others,
exuberance about life, serenity. We develop a willingness to stick with things,
a sense of compassion in the heart, and a conviction that a basic holiness
permeates things and people. We find ourselves involved in loyal commitments,
not needing to force our way in life, able to marshal and direct our energies
wisely.*

1. Underline what happens when we try to get things our way.

2. Circle what happens when we do things God's way.

3. Would you agree God is giving us a choice?

4. What's hard about doing it God's way?

5. What do you think cheap sex means? How is it avoidable?

Proverbs 29:16 Keep the rules and keep your life; careless living kills.

Rules, sort of an annoying word - but what do you think the point of them is for?

_____

_____

_____

Truth: He has your best interest and He designed you the way you are (no mistakes).
Your beliefs don't change the truth.
But your beliefs do change how you respond to the truth.

Do you believe God has your best interest? Why or Why not?

_____

_____

_____

[END OF STUDY]

[END OF STUDY]

HEALTHY BOUNDARIES

BY JESSE TAURA

Dating 3.5 years and "scared to death of the thought of kissing. Fast-forward a couple of months and we had the kissing thing down pat (I'll spare you the awkward details of the beginning). Let's just say our boundaries were formed in an unintentional sort of way. We would find ourselves often kissing in a car. Late. At night. Hmm… we finally thought…we have to

wasn't thinking about sex, and honestly I never thought I would. The struggle is definitely real. Just be aware, it's out there, and that's okay. More importantly, the desire for intimacy is essential for a healthy relationship.

2. Practice - not always perfect
You may be at either end of the spectrum; experienced or so naïve it ain't funny. It's very easy to be misguided when it comes to boundaries, regardless of your experience level. Don't be fooled: being inexperienced doesn't protect you just as much as been-there-done-that doesn't make you anymore trustworthy.

KNOW WHERE YOU STAND – Don't rely on your bf or gf to call the shots. Regardless of your past

TALKING IS KEY IN A RELATIONSHIP. IF YOU DON'T TALK, YOUR THOUGHTS ‑ NOT YOUR CONVICTIONS ‑ WILL DICTATE YOUR ACTIONS.

work out boundaries. I quickly decided mine and shared them with Him. "Hey, let's not kiss late at night in a car. That way we won't push any boundaries. It wasn't long before we found ourselves making out before the sun came up at 5:30am as I was dropping him to work.

1. The struggle is real
If you are in / or one day will be in a relationship, it is likely you will struggle with pushing boundaries. Most (if not all) people do, it is part of being a human and experiencing the real desires that God has put in each of us. But for most of us, there is a period of waiting. If you have never thought about sex in your life, you will. Because I wasn't in a relationship, I

experiences (or lack of) decide what your boundaries are and get help from someone older who you respect and can help you make wise choices. Decide for yourself, discuss together and communicate early on.

BE AWARE – Be knowledgeable when it comes to sex. Look to the right places and people. There are so many voices out there competing for your attention. You choose the right ones; they will help guide you to make healthy choices.

3. Communicate
Talking is key in a relationship. If you don't talk, your thoughts – not your convictions - will dictate your actions. A relationship (especially early on) is about pleasing each other. There's

nothing wrong with this, this is a really fun part of a relationship - For us intimacy was the same, but outside of marriage we needed to take a few steps of caution.

TALK ABOUT YOUR EXPECTATIONS – make it known what you are expecting when it comes to intimacy (this could help you determine if he/she is a fit for you)

TALK ABOUT YOUR FEARS – It is possible that fear could be driving you to do things you don't want to do. Fear of rejection or maybe the fear of rejecting as well.

4. Striving is not arriving

The thing is, we were not created to do anything in our own strength. For a long time this is something I tried to do. If I got

ASK THE SPIRIT – guilt will not be you motivator. It cannot help you. Ask the spirit of God to fill you - it only takes a thought.

5. Assess and make changes

Like I said earlier let God speak to you individually about your boundaries (See note 2). What I will say is, don't have the assumption that this statement will be the cure for your boundaries. Remember any boundary that you set, prepare for it to be challenged. Listing all your aims will not be the end of this journey.

BUDGET FOR SUCCESS - So you might stuff up. But, rather than throwing the boundaries out the window, it can be helpful to spend some time re-evaluating. For an example, a goal: Spend time in a

REMEMBER ANY BOUNDARY THAT YOU SET, PREPARE FOR IT TO BE CHALLENGED.

it wrong (which I definitely did many times), I would try to do it better and be better. The problem with this was, I blamed myself, my lack of self-control and for my lapse of judgment. The Bible says, 'good works done in the flesh, brings death'[1]. Attempting to "do good" in the flesh is called striving. When we strive, we grow tired and less able to actually have self-control. Striving is our attempt to conquer our weaknesses independently of the God and The Holy Spirit. This will only hurt you. In your time of need, pray, call on the Holy Spirit and His help will bring life.

group -if you are realistic this may not have always been an option. If last week you found yourself alone watching a movie because all of your housemates or family were "out", decide to go for a walk together, be about in public. You don't need to be absolutely positively, and completely alone to be able to spend some personal time.

Healthy (S)ex pectations

BY SAMANTHA BENNETTS

SEX IS AWKWARD.

Imagine two dancers coming together to perform a pas de deux - a choreographed dance for two people - without any practice - without even knowing the choreography beforehand. Limbs flailing, bodies moving, missed cues and misread signals. Heart rates are up and everything's a little out

things you'd like to try, things that make you uncomfortable. If you can't vocalize it don't expect to get it. And if you can't encourage your partner to be open and vulnerable too, don't expect to be able to please them sexually.

SEX IS MESSY

You know that scene in the movie - the one you feel really awkward watching with your parents? Yeah, the sex scene. Think about how it ends. The guy and the girl have sex, finish up, and maybe they get up, put their clothes on and get back to their lives. Or maybe they cuddle, roll over, and go to sleep. Hollywood leaves a fair bit out here because sex is messy. And if it wasn't it wouldn't be any good. Often, there's sweat involved. Liquids are shooting around. There'll be some clean up.

It's not just for pleasure. Sex is about intimacy and vulnerability and that makes it a powerful force in a relationship.

of time. Feel the awkwardness? Now imagine doing all of that naked. Now imagine doing all of that with furniture involved. This can be a little like sex for the first time. Yeah, you're welcome. The point is - don't expect it be a seamlessly choreographed dance of passion the first time (or first few times) around. Have fun, giggle communicate and don't take yourself too seriously.

SEX IS VULNERABLE

In a mutually loving and trusting sexual relationship, you're putting yourself and your body on the line. You're baring all (literally), and yeah, it can take a little while to get used to. Sex will only be 'good' if you embrace the vulnerability. Real intimacy requires real vulnerability and trust, from both sides of the table. Communicate about what you like and dislike,

It's not always as glamorous as they make it out to be.

SEX IS POWERFUL

When you spend a long time trying not to have sex, like if you've decided to wait until marriage, it can set the focus on the physical urge. The pleasure element. Which is important, for sure. But sex is not just about a 'release'. It's not just for pleasure. Sex is about intimacy and vulnerability and that makes it a powerful force in a relationship. During and after sex, your body releases the hormones Oxytocin and Vasopressin, which create deepening bonds of attachment, protectiveness and devotion. Just like open and honest communication, quality time, shared goals and values, sex is a powerful tool in building and maintaining a healthy and devoted relationship.

BUT YOU WON'T ALWAYS FEEL LIKE HAVING SEX

"But you don't understand, my sex drive is through the roof. When we get married, I'll be wanting it 24/7." Again, resisting the temptation to have sex can give you an unrealistic idea of your sex drive. The wanting can be exacerbated by the denial. This is important because once you're in a sexual relationship, and are in it for a while, you realise sex is influenced by other factors, not just your hormones. What kind of day you had, tiredness, stress, how much you've interacted with your partner that day, romance (or lack thereof), your health, the list goes on. Someone once said, "Sex starts in the kitchen" and there's truth in that. It's important to cultivate sexual desire, not just expect it to happen open dialogue with friends, parents or mentors about sex, but the most important dialogue is between you and your partner. When you decide to get married, people will give you all kinds of advice - which is great - but remember that your partnership is unique and your experiences will be as well. Don't compare, don't try too hard to imitate, and don't judge your performance based on another person's experiences.

SEX IS GOOD!

And if at first it's not? That's ok. But it shouldn't stay that way. Real intimacy, trust and vulnerability means that when it's not good, it's ok to talk about it, to seek advice, to educate yourselves and work together to make it good - for both of you. Don't expect it to be good straight away - you're trying to do

Don't expect it to be good straight away - you're trying to do a seamlessly synchronized dance and you've never practiced the steps.

the way it did when you started out. It becomes about the fact that you did the dishes that morning, the surprise coffee in bed, the phone call just to say "I love you", the weeknight take out you treated yourselves to, the hand that held on just a split second longer before letting go. And no, this is not just the case for women. Sometimes you have to work for a healthy sexual relationship, and that's ok.

SEX IS PERSONAL

Nowadays we are told all the time that we are unique - unique fingerprints, unique body types, unique in our minds and our thinking. When a couple comes together it is the joining of two unique individuals to create a completely unique partnership… So don't expect your sexual experience to be the same as anyone else's. It's great to have an a seamlessly synchronized dance and you've never practiced the steps. Just like a relationship, you have to work to have good sex, so expect to work for it. Be prepared to be vulnerable enough to work for it. Don't settle. Don't give up.

STI'S/ CONTRA-CEPTION

"DON'T HAVE SEX, BECAUSE YOU WILL GET PREGNANT AND DIE! DON'T HAVE SEX IN THE MISSIONARY POSITION, DON'T HAVE SEX STANDING UP, JUST DON'T DO IT, OK, PROMISE? OK, NOW EVERYBODY TAKE SOME RUBBERS."

— COACH CARR, MEAN GIRLS

STI - SEXUALLY TRANSMITTED INFECTION.

SELF EXPLANATORY, BODILY FLUIDS CAN BE EXCHANGED DURING ANY SEXUAL ACTIVITY (NOT JUST INTERCOURSE), RESULTING IN A SEXUALLY TRANSMITTED INFECTION. THEY ARE COMMON AND SOME ARE TREATABLE. IF NOT TREATED THEY CAN CAUSE LONG-TERM EFFECTS. 1/4 PEOPLE WILL GET ONE IN THEIR LIFETIME. 13 MILLION IN THE US A YEAR ARE DIAGNOSED 65% OF PEOPLE WITH AN STI ARE UNDER THE AGE OF 25. MOST COMMON INFECTIONS (US AND AUS): CHLAMYDIA / GONORRHEA / SYPHILIS / (HIV) AND AIDS / GENITAL WARTS (HERPES) / HPV

DID YOU KNOW: THERE ISN'T A CURE FOR HERPES, 56% OF SEXUALLY ACTIVE PEOPLE DON'T KNOW THAT.

THE NUMBER OF PEOPLE BEING INFECTED WITH HIV HAS INCREASED BY 10%.

WE'RE NOT INVINCIBLE, ANYONE CAN GET AN STI, IT'S VERY COMMON TO THINK "IT WON'T HAPPEN TO ME". THAT THINKING EXPLAINS WHY SO MANY YOUNG PEOPLE TAKE UNHEALTHY RISKS.

THE STATS ARE CLEAR 39% OF SEXUALLY ACTIVE STUDENTS REPORTED THEY ONLY USED CONDOMS 'SOMETIMES' WHEN THEY HAD SEX, AND 13% NEVER USED CONDOMS. THE RESOURCES TO BE PROTECTED ARE AVAILABLE.

IF YOU'RE DOING IT, YOU NEED TO GET TESTED. SIGNS/SYMPTOMS ARE NOT ALWAYS VISIBLE.

CONDOMS ARE THE BEST FORM OF PROTECTION FROM STI'S.

CONTRACEPTION I.E. HOW TO NOT GET PREGNANT.

HERE IS A BRIEF LIST, BUT A PERSON CONSIDERING THESE NEEDS TO TALK TO THEIR HEALTHCARE PROVIDER TO DETERMINE THE BEST FIT FOR THEM.

CHOOSING NOT TO HAVE SEX / BIRTH CONTROL PILLS / CONDOMS / THE RING / IUD, IF SOMEONE IS USING BIRTH CONTROL, YOU STILL NEED A CONDOM TO PROTECT FROM STI'S.

Make the decision for yourself - you'll have to reaffirm this regularly

Avoid situations where it will be hard to stick to the decision

Avoid alcohol and drugs – they can mess with your judgment

Find people who you can talk about it with – lean on their support

Talk about it with your bf/gf before you're in the heat of the moment

Be straightforward with your boundaries/limits

Keep in mind that sex is a good thing*

*A lot of Christian couples struggle with feeling guilty about having sex - even in marriage - because they told themselves sex was ONLY good in marriage. Just because you sign a marriage certificate doesn't change your mindset. It's okay to desire sex, it's okay to talk about sex, having a healthy MINDSET will help sex in marriage.

WHILE YOU WAIT

(n.)
1. The philosophy of talking candidly and openly and honestly
without fear of what others might think_

a. Usually for another's benefit to let them know of something that
is usually hard to discuss[2].

REAL TALK.

AN INTERVIEW WITH SARAH M.

AGE: 17

HOBBY/S: Geez, I have so many, I thoroughly enjoy National Geographic magazines. I love art and making 'stuff'. I love going to art galleries. I don't mind a good read. I like shopping in second hand clothing stores (because it's all I can afford and I generally find hidden treasures). I honestly love hanging out with my brothers (I have three). I love the beach. I love eating in general (fruit and ice cream, Nutella, burgers and pizza) - sick diet I know. I also love being surrounded by my mates.

FAV SONG/MOVIE: This is a tough one. There are so many movies I like so, if I were to narrow down to a favourite song it would have to be, Blood Bank, Bon Iver OR Cavalier, James Vincent McMorrow. But my favourite songs are always changing and are determined based on what mood I'm in.

Stance on sex life? (where do you stand, i.e. having sex or not and why?) Personally I have never been into that kind of "stuff". I'm abnormally quite mature for my age as well as stubborn, especially when it comes to relationships - I haven't always been like that, but right now I can say, as a teenager, I have no interest in having sex (right now), drinking or smoking etc. I guess I've been brought up to know that sex was made for marriage but I think it comes down to the individual's convictions, personal values and opinions. I'm not really sure how to describe my stance on sex well - but I think a lot of it can come down to insecurities and what feels good at the time. It's a fact that teenagers and even young adults are lead by their feelings and so there's an abundance of temptation and perhaps irrational thinking when it comes to having sex. I guess because I'm comfortable with who I am, having sex now seems a little unnecessary. I'm happy to wait purely because I don't really care what others think of me, I'm okay with waiting and I think others should feel okay about that as well.

Friends influences? Are you cool with talking to your friends about sex, regardless of difference of opinions (how do you navigate that)?

I guess surrounding yourself with really good friends who have similar values to you are so good to have. It can be hard to find friends like that but they're out there, I promise. When I talk to my friends about it, I feel pretty comfortable. We're all usually on the same page but I guess if I'm talking to one of my friends who don't really understand or who have different views on sex, I think it is important to be empathetic, understanding and non-judgmental. I think it's okay for people to have different views on sex, I think it's more important to love the person based on who they are rather than their actions because I believe that placing value on people is far greater than pointing out their flaws (that's not our job anyways). I believe that being someone who listens to people and who genuinely care about what the person is saying, not only says a lot about you, but also says so much about the God we serve. He loves, He cares and He listens. So, I think it's important to be real with people because it makes you more relatable. I try to be as honest as I can because sometimes getting vulnerable in front of people lets others know that they're not alone and that their problems aren't silly or unfixable, but rather small hiccups that will pass eventually.

How do you honour God with your sexuality? Why is this important to you? (Also you were passionate about sex being talked about in a positive way at church- mention that)

In terms of honouring God with my sexuality, I think I've learnt (and am still learning) to trust God with this. Arguably, I have little life experience, but I have enough to know where I stand with sex, that is, to wait until I'm married. I formed these convictions when I was very young, as I've seen very close family members fall apart from abusing substances, alcohol and sex. It didn't scare me, it didn't make me love them any less, it just broadened my perspective on the world and the importance of looking after ourselves, valuing sex and respecting our bodies.

So much of what I value comes from the way I've been brought up and also the church environment I've grown up in. I'm so blessed to have parents who have been open about sex, who have been so accepting and humble in the way they love and serve others in the general public. I'm also, incredibly blessed to have grown up in a church that places value on the next generations, who are open about healthy relationships and sex. I think it's so necessary for churches and parents to not be fearful or condemning of the subject but rather embrace it and be an example to those who don't understand or value it. Times are changing rapidly and I think some churches and parents need to catch up and raise their kids up to be teenagers and adults who aren't scared of sex, but who understand the value of it and who respect and love others who don't yet have that understanding.

INSIDE OUT.

By Sam Fagan

The past has passed.
Your self-worth is NOT based on your sexual choices.

I'm about to make a huge sweeping statement. I hope you still like me after this. Can we all agree up front, before we go any further, that no one is perfect? What! How dare you. Don't box me. You don't know me like that homie.

For reals though. TBH.

We have all done something we wish we hadn't. A mistake. A moment we wish we could get back. A choice we regret. Have you ever said to yourself "I messed up."? Well, it happens to the best of us.

With the daily pressures of family, faith, friends, the media, not to mention my own internal expectations... It's not a question of 'Will I make a mistake', but more like 'when will I'?

Thanks for the positive message! :) Stay with me.

The good news is that you don't have to pretend like you have it all together. The pressure is off. You don't have to be perfect because nobody is. What a relief! I can just be myself. Flaws and all. I'm accepted and I have value because we all are anything but the highlight reel we project on social media.

Your worth is not determined by how perfect your life is. It's deeper than that. Your worth is not found in the external things; it's the internal things that matter. Your worth is not found or measured in how good or bad you have been up to this point, because you are more than your behaviour.
"People look at the outward appearance, but the Lord looks at the heart." – 1 Samuel 16:7 (NLT)

With this understanding, can I tell you the truth about your SEXUALITY?
You are NOT your mistakes; you are NOT your past. And it's ok if you don't have a perfect track record. You are valuable because of who you are, not what you do.

So if your sexual past has been a heavy weight on your shoulders, a constant headache in your mind, or a small voice telling you you'll never get past what you've done or what has been done to you... You're accepted anyway. Loved unconditionally. You belong. Your past has passed and your future looks incredible!

How? Why? The answer is Jesus. He is that good. We don't deserve it. But He offers His love and acceptance; He gives it to you. Despite your decisions regarding your sexuality and regardless of your history, because of Jesus we can move past what we've done. We can experience freedom in our hearts and minds, and we can know that our true value isn't in our sexual choices, it's found in a friendship with Jesus. He loves you unconditionally, just as you are. And He has a great plan and purpose for your life.

Learn from mistakes.
Make the right choice next time.
Don't be defined by your past.
Be defined by Jesus.
Discover His love.
It's better than any other love.

What is the good in the bad?
What can you learn from it?

People look at the outward appearance but the Lord looks at the heart. 1 Samuel 167 NLT

Handwritten background text:
LOVE YOU, babe, so bad, so bad
AINT ... Y, CAN
get ... ith m
love ... d, bal
et's ... oldin
na ... so ba

AM 12:25
JUN. 09 2016

COUPLE STORY.
SHAYLA & JOSH.

SHAYLA: 20 & JOSH: 21
TOGETHER: 4 YEARS

First Kiss.
S: (her first kiss ever) He walked me to my door and just did, I was so nervous.
J: (Josh started young, first kiss was in kindy).

Favorite quality about each other?
S: He is ridiculously funny and caring!
J: I love/hate her independence! It's what honestly attracted me the most to her, after her smile of course ha! I love how she doesn't need approval or is reliant on people. She knows what she wants (except when it comes to food) and she knows who she is! She didn't need me to tell her her worth or what she should value. It's definitely my favourite thing about Shay but also is the most frustrating at times ha-ha.

Favorite date:
S: We went to the Easter show- spent so much time together, he spent lots of money on me, (she giggles), went on high roller coasters, which he hates, but for me. he did.
J: Sydney Royal Easter Show '10. I'm terrified of heights! But she loves the rush, so I went on all of the rides I'd NEVER EVER EVER go on just to impress her ha-ha! We had the best time!

Chill time looks like?
S: We like to go out to eat, go to the drive-ins, hang out with friends a lot.
J: Movies!! Any and every...it's our thing! We recently just started going to the drive in cinemas...it's the best! Followed by KFC :).

Having sex? No.
Why/Why not?
S: I value him, I love him, it's how I show my love to him. I believe in the dreams God has given him and I don't want to compromise that.
J: Because we're not married yet. It's crazy. As a young teenager before me and Shay were together, I honestly had my moments. I had done everything under the sun except sex. I wanted to wait for the 'one'. I

found her. But I had found Jesus first. And how lucky am I, she knew Jesus also! It worked out well. Our values lined up right from the start and as Christian, purity is a value you NEED to have. Right from the start our values lined up, so I knew that she was the one! It's a conversation that you'll need to have if you're serious about the relationship you're in!

Do you find it difficult?
J: IT IS SO HARD! I mean, at the end of the day I'm human. So being a young teenager/adult my hormones are going nuts ha-ha-ha! Plus I'm attracted to her not only emotionally but physically as well LOL. I think what makes it hardest, is the world we live in today. Sex is everywhere. Is so accessible and it's even in the music we listen to. Society hasn't made it easy especially when everyone around you is doing it. You've got to know what you believe and not let them (the world) decide what you do.

How has this choice shaped your relationship? (view of each other, future?)
S: It puts value on it, we focus on other things, which bring vision that I don't want to jeopardise. I feel this decision hasn't just shaped our relationship, it's shaped us as individuals. It has made everything I do, whether church or work or college, prioritise Jesus; to make sure that He is at the centre of all I do, not me, because I can't do this on my own - it's impossible. It needs to come from a place in your own life. Putting God first in your life and then letting Him be the focus in every other area of your life. How would you define the culture of your relationship? Willingness to release each other to do what God has called us to do (not getting offended if we can't always hang). Being real with feelings (like stuff we're embarrassed to say).
J: It's taken time but I love that we've got to a place where it's not about our individual needs or wants but it's all about her for me and me for her. It's crazy I've

just realised this now, but she's actually so supportive of me and in everything I do. I like to think that I'm the same (I try to make sure ha) but I'm all about her crushing life, achieving her goals and dreams and I'm backing her!!!

Family supportive?
S: Our families are so different, but they try.
J: Absolutely! My parents love Shay but most importantly my siblings love her and get along with her. I'm pretty sure she's closer to them than I am ha.

Friends supportive?
S: Yes! We hang in groups often.
J: My friends love Shayla! Never ever heard anything bad come from them about her, I mean come on...it's Shay. What's not to love! Ha-ha.

Who do you talk to about your relationship?
S: Yeah, I talk to girls who are a bit older than I am and in relationships for advice.
J: I have a few people in my life, mainly my leaders and close friends who themselves are in relationships or married - so they understand and can relate and have experience.

Advice for couples dating?
S: Be open and talk to people you trust about your relationship - be open to advice and growing.
J: Before even thinking about dating or relationships, figure out what are your core values. Ask yourself-what do you believe? Where do you want to go? Where's God taking you? From there you'll be able to gauge whether or not you are on the right track and you'll know whether you are ready for a relationship or not. I mean if you can't first lead yourself, how can you lead in a relationship? However, if that's all on lock, your values should line up with your partner. If they don't, you may need to re-evaluate the relationship and where you guys are heading.

SEXUAL ABUSE

There always seems to be a guilty feeling, a shameful feeling or a feeling of secrecy related to abuse. Especially when it comes to sexual abuse. It's puzzling to think that I'm not talking about the person who abuses, but the one who experiences the abuse.

The guilt might be because we think we are strong enough to stop it. The self-blame might be because you think 'Did I put myself in this situation?'. The secrecy might be because you think you didn't say no or because you were told to keep a secret. The shame might be because it felt good when he or she was touching me... because biologically that is a natural response when someone touches our sexual organs.

You were the victim in the situation, you were the one that was abused by the abuser, they were the one that did the wrong thing, not you. Remember that you cannot control another person's actions or decisions.

There are things that we can't control, like predicting what is going to happen or turning back the clock; however a person's actions are something they can control and your abuser chose to not control their actions. **Every human being deserves dignity, respect and a right to choose and your abuser robbed you of these basic rights.**

It helps to speak up about the stuff that you have experienced, especially if this includes a traumatic experience - because getting through sexual abuse is hard enough, let alone dealing with all the guilt, shame and self-blame that can come with it.

— Jo Madison

TO *THROW* THE *STONE.*

The Pharisees brought Jesus a woman who had committed adultery (cheating when you're married), in that time her actions would have got her stoned to death, instead Jesus made a huge statement with her life. "Jesus bent down and wrote with his finger in the dirt. They kept at him, badgering him. He straightened up and said,"The sinless one among you, go first: Throw the stone." Bending down again, he wrote some more in the dirt. Hearing that, they walked away, one after another, beginning with the oldest. The woman was left alone. Jesus stood up and spoke to her. "Woman, where are they? Does no one condemn you?" "No one, Master.""Neither do I," said Jesus. "Go on your way. From now on, don't sin." – John 8:1-11 (MSG)

God is full of grace and at the same time He corrects us. He sent her away forgiven, but asked her to change.

You are not your mistakes. Your worth isn't defined by your sexual choices.

Most of us have done some things we're not too proud of, but scriptures show us we can be forgiven. Guilt doesn't have to control you.

If you do have that conviction inside telling you not to do something, follow that. It's your values speaking ⁃ if you stuff up, cool, get up and keep trying, God doesn't hold it against you; but you can't keep repeating the same thing.

YOUNG, WILD AND FREE
YOUNG, WILD AND FREE
YOUNG, WILD AND FREE
YOUNG, WILD AND FREE
YOUNG, WILD AND FREE
YOUNG, WILD AND FREE
YOUNG, WILD AND FREE
YOUNG, WILD AND FREE
YOUNG, WILD AND FREE
YOUNG, WILD AND FREE
YOUNG, WILD AND FREE
YOUNG, WILD AND FREE

YOUNG, WILD AND FREE
YOUNG, WILD AND FREE
YOUNG, WILD AND FREE
YOUNG, WILD AND FREE
YOUNG, WILD AND FREE
YOUNG, WILD AND FREE
YOUNG, WILD AND FREE
YOUNG, WILD AND FREE
YOUNG, WILD AND FREE
YOUNG, WILD AND FREE
YOUNG, WILD AND FREE
YOUNG, WILD AND FREE
YOUNG, WILD AND FREE
YOUNG, WILD AND FREE
YOUNG, WILD AND FREE
YOUNG, WILD AND FREE
YOUNG, WILD AND FREE
YOUNG, WILD AND FREE
YOUNG, WILD AND FREE
YOUNG, WILD AND FREE
YOUNG, WILD AND FREE
YOUNG, WILD AND FREE
YO   *FREE*
YO   *FREE*
YO   *FREE*
YO   *FREE*
YO   *FREE*
YO   *FREE*
YO   *FREE*
YO   *FREE*
YO   *FREE*
YOUNG, WILD AND FREE
YOUNG, WILD AND FREE

THE SEX REVOLUTION

WHO: HIPPIES IN CALIFORNIA

WHEN: DURING THE 60-70'S

WHAT: SEX WAS NOT A THING PEOPLE DISCUSSED. THE WORD 'SEX' CARRIED PAIN, SHAME, JUDGMENT AND CONFUSION, TO THE POINT WHERE IT WAS FROWNED UPON FOR WOMEN TO SAY THEY ENJOYED SEX (LIKE... SERIOUSLY?).

WHY: PEOPLE STARTED TO VIEW SEX AS AN EXPRESSION OF LOVE, A PHYSICAL PLEASURE, AND SOMETHING TO BE CELEBRATED!

WHAT IT MEANS FOR US TODAY:

A DIVIDE BETWEEN

SEXUAL EMPOWERMENT SAYS ALL PEOPLE SHOULD BE CONFIDENT AND COMFORTABLE WITH THEIR BODIES, HAVE THE RIGHT TO HOLISTIC SEX EDUCATION, WE SHOULD BE ABLE TO ENJOY SEX, EROTICA SHOULD BE NORMALIZED AND NOT REPRESSED.

SEXUAL OBJECTIFICATION IS SEEING OR TREATING A PERSON AS IF THEY ARE AN OBJECT; SINGLING OUT A WOMAN'S BODY OR THE BODY OF THE PERSON - MAKING THAT PERSON JUST AN OBJECT (USUALLY FOR MALE SEXUAL DESIRE).

BUT BECAUSE OF THE MEDIA, THE TWO ARE OFTEN CONFUSED.

OVER-SEXUALISED IMAGES IN THE MEDIA TEACHES BOTH SEXES THAT VALUE AND WORTH COMES FROM SEX APPEAL.

ACTOR (AND FORMER SEX ADDICT) RUSSELL BRAND IN A BLOG[3] URGES PEOPLE TO "ADDRESS OUR OBSESSION WITH LOOKING AT WOMEN RATHER THAN INTERACTING WITH THEM" AND THINKS THIS QUESTION IS WORTH CONSIDERING, "HOW CAN WE UNDERSTAND OUR SEXUALITY? HOW CAN WE EXPRESS IT LOVINGLY IN HARMONY WITH THE PRINCIPLES THAT IT'S THERE TO DEMONSTRATE PROCREATION AND SENSUAL LOVE BETWEEN CONSENTING ADULTS?"

SEXUAL EMPOWERMENT IS A HUMAN RIGHT - IT AFFECTS BOTH BOYS AND GIRLS AND THEREFORE NEEDS BOTH SEXES TO WORK TOWARDS IT. HOWEVER, IT CAN BE HARD TO TELL IF SOMETHING IS SEXUALLY EMPOWERING OR OBJECTIFYING.

THE WINNING FACTOR IS WHO HAS THE POWER.

WE ARE CONSTANTLY GIVEN SEXUALISED IMAGES OF GIRLS AND BOYS THROUGH ADVERTISING, MERCHANDISING, MUSIC, VIDEO GAMES AND ALL FORMS OF MEDIA.

THE RESULT IS THAT MANY PEOPLE STRUGGLE WITH BODY IMAGE, SELF-ESTEEM, EMOTIONAL EFFECTS AND DEPRESSION RATES AND THERE ARE MENTAL AND PHYSICAL CONSEQUENCES DUE TO THE EFFECTS OF THE MEDIA.

THE TAKEAWAY HERE IS SIMPLY TO QUESTION EVERYTHING YOU'RE VIEWING - HOW DOES THIS MAKE ME FEEL ABOUT MYSELF? HOW IS THIS SAYING I SHOULD BE TREATED? HOW IS IT SHAPING MY EXPECTATIONS?

FOR EXAMPLE, ASKING YOURSELF NOT JUST WHAT THE LYRICS TO YOUR FAVOURITE SONGS MEAN, BUT HOW THEY AFFECT YOUR THINKING.

Killa

TEMPTATION IS A DESIRE TO DO SOMETHING
USUALLY UNWISE AND WRONG.

KEY WORD HERE, DESIRE (STRONG FEELING OF
WANTING SOMETHING).

SO, THE ISSUE (PERSON, SITUATION) WE'RE
FACING IS NOT THE TEMPTER, BUT THE DESIRE IS
AND WHAT CHOICE WE MAKE.

AN 'ISSUE' COULD BE DEBATING TO HAVE SEX,
STAYING THE NIGHT OVER BF OR GF HOUSE, LYING
TO YOUR PARENTS, ETC.

DESIRES COME FROM OUR HEART AND THOUGHT
LIFE.

THE BIBLE TELLS US THAT TEMPTATION IS
MANAGEABLE.
1 CORINTHIANS 10:13 SAYS THAT NO TEST OR
TEMPTATION THAT COMES YOUR WAY IS BEYOND THE
COURSE OF WHAT OTHERS HAVE HAD TO FACE. ALL
YOU NEED TO REMEMBER IS THAT GOD WILL NEVER
LET YOU DOWN; HE'LL NEVER LET YOU BE PUSHED
PAST YOUR LIMIT; HE'LL ALWAYS BE THERE TO
HELP YOU COME THROUGH IT.

AND THAT WE CAN CONTROL OUR THOUGHT LIFE.
WE CAN DO THIS BY THINKING BIG PICTURE,
BEING INTENTIONAL ABOUT WHAT YOU ARE
'FEEDING' YOURSELF (MOVIES, MUSIC,
MAGAZINES). YOU CAN ACTUALLY SPEAK SCRIPTURE
INTO YOUR SITUATION (FIND A SCRIPTURE
THAT RELATES TO WHAT YOU ARE DEALING WITH
AND MEDITATE ON THAT). ALSO, CONSIDER THE
MESSAGES YOUR FRIENDS ARE TELLING YOU - ARE
THEY POSITIVE OR NEGATIVE VIBE?

**IT ISN'T A SIN TO BE TEMPTED (SO DON'T FEEL
GUILTY); IT'S ONLY A SIN IF YOU ACT ON THE
TEMPTATION - (EVEN JESUS WAS TEMPTED).**

PARENTAL
ADVISORY
EXPLICIT CONTENT

BLURRED LINES.

MYTH BUSTERS

B/C THANKS TO THE MOVIES AND THE HOMIES THERE HAS BEEN SOME CONFUSION.

¿¿¿?

1. FOOT SIZE TELLS US PENIS SIZE:

A recent study on penis sizes tells us the opposite. There is no connection between foot size and penis size[4].

2. PORN TEACHES US HOW TO HAVE SEX:

Nope, nope, nope! We never see the awkwardness of putting on condoms, or that it can take 45 minutes of foreplay for a girl to be fully sexually aroused, no funny noises, no protection, no emotions or intimacy.

3. EVERYONE IS DOING IT:

Almost three quarters of Year 10 students (77%), third of Year 11 students (34%) and one-half of Year 12 students (50%) haven't experienced sexual intercourse[5].

5. ORAL SEX IS SAFER SEX:

Quite simply no, still at risk for STI's and there can be emotional repercussion as well.

6. YOU HAVE TO TRY BEFORE YOU BUY:

Relationships aren't about how good you are physically, but the intimacy that grows between two partners, the more open and honest you are with each other the more fun it will be. You don't have to have several partners or 'try before you buy' to make sure that person is the "right one". Sex is different between any two people, it takes time to understand your body and your partners, to figure out what you like and don't like- it's a journey.

7. YOU CAN TELL IF SOMEONE HAS AN STI BY LOOKING AT THEM:

Sometimes signs are not noticeable.

8. GOD HATES SEX:

If there is one thing this study screams, it's that God created sex and says it is good. The New Testament even talks about married couples needing to do it!_

9. SEX LIFE IS OVER ONCE YOU GET MARRIED:

Sex is actually more satisfying in a committed relationship and more frequent! Sex in the City, Entourage, music videos tell us there's just seas of people to sleep with, but in reality your desires are more likely to be met with that significant other.

10. SEX LAST FOR HOURS:

Actually, it is more like 6-8 minutes on average (even shorter time is normal for men with erectile issues). P to V penetration 6-10 min over all 30-50 min (including foreplay).

11. SEX IS A DAILY ACTIVITY:

It's different for everyone and quality over quantity is more important.

12. MEN ALWAYS WANT SEX:

The pressure of that - geez, men do get sleepy, do get sick, do get stressed etc. Men and women both have this belief and that actually puts pressure on men to perform- when it's okay for them to not want 'it' all the time.

WHEN A LOT OF PEOPLE HEAR THAT WORD 'MASTURBATION' THEY THINK PORN, BUT IT'S IMPORTANT TO DISCONNECT THE TWO.

THERE IS A LOT OF HISTORY WHEN IT COMES TO THIS SUBJECT; LOTS OF BELIEFS, LOTS OF OPINIONS.

IT'S NOT A BLACK AND WHITE ISSUE, AND THIS IS WHY IT HAS CAUSED CONTROVERSY FOR CENTURIES. IT'S TIME WE CRITICALLY THINK ABOUT IT AND UNDERSTAND NOT ONLY WHAT IT IS, BUT WHAT IT DOES.

PAST GENERATIONS WERE TAUGHT THAT MASTURBATION CAUSED BLINDNESS, MENTAL ILLNESS AND EVEN HAIRY PALMS.

MASTUR

BIT OF A TOUCHY SUBJECT, HA.

SERIOUSLY? WE CAN ACTUALLY TRACE BACK THE NEGATIVE VIEWS AROUND MASTURBATING TO THE VICTORIAN AGE WHERE IT WAS CONSIDERED A SIN AND PEOPLE WERE MADE TO BELIEVE IT WOULD BRING DISEASES! SOCIETY LATCHED ONTO THIS, BOTH IN RELIGIOUS AND NON-RELIGIOUS SPHERES, AND IT'S BEEN 'BAD' SINCE THEN.

IT'S IMPORTANT TO PUSH PAST THE FEAR OF TALKING ABOUT THESE IFFY TOPICS AND CHALLENGE THEM TOGETHER.

STILL, THERE IS MUCH SHAME ATTACHED TO MASTURBATION. OBVIOUSLY, IF IT'S A HABIT

LIKE ANY OTHER IT CAN BE UNHEALTHY AND DESTRUCTIVE IF DISTORTED.

PEOPLE OFTEN FEEL GUILT FROM BELIEFS ABOUT MASTURBATION (PRESSURE FROM CHURCH, SOCIETY, OR MAYBE FAMILY), RATHER THAN MASTURBATION IN ITSELF.

THE STATS FOR YOUNG PEOPLE MASTURBATING ARE HIGH. THIS IS PROOF THAT IT IS NORMAL. IF YOU HAVE DONE IT, WHETHER YOU ARE A BOY OR A GIRL, THERE IS NO NEED TO FEEL LIKE A FREAK.

DON'T WORRY ABOUT IT TOO MUCH; JUST BE CAREFUL THAT IT DOESN'T 'OVERTAKE YOU'.

ALL RIGHT, SO WE HAVE THIS SITUATION: GOD SAYS SEX IS GOOD – SEXUAL DESIRES ARE NATURAL. THE BIBLE DOESN'T EVEN ACTUALLY MENTION MASTURBATION, SO NOWHERE DOES IT SAY IT IS A SIN.

FROM THIS, WE CAN CONCLUDE IT IS NOT A SIN ~~ BUT JESUS SAYS "LOOKING WITH LUST" IS A SIN.

SO, THE QUESTION IS CAN YOU MASTURBATE WITHOUT LUSTING?

IT IS NEARLY IMPOSSIBLE TO MASTURBATE WITHOUT FANTASY, BUT IT CAN BE DONE. THERE AREN'T STATS ABOUT THAT, BUT I'VE ASKED AROUND (YES, IT WAS AWKWARD,

BATION

IF IT IS SOMETHING YOU THINK YOU COULD BE STRUGGLING WITH (TAKES UP LOTS OF YOUR TIME, CAUSES YOU TO LIE, DOING IT WHILE WATCHING PORN) THEN YOU SHOULD SEEK HELP FROM SOMEONE.

MEDICALLY, THERE IS NO EVIDENCE THAT MASTURBATING IS HARMFUL.

BUT WHY DO PEOPLE DO IT? MASTURBATING CAN BE SELF-SOOTHING; A WAY TO RELAX AND RELEASE SEXUAL TENSIONS. SOME PEOPLE TO DO IT TO UNDERSTAND THEIR BODY BETTER AND TO LEARN WHAT GIVES THEM PLEASURE.

BUT I NEEDED TO KNOW IF PEOPLE FOUND THAT POSSIBLE).

NOTE: PORN IS VERY HARMFUL TO THE WIRING OF THE BRAIN AND TO SOCIETY. USING PORN TO MASTURBATE IS UNHEALTHY. WE'LL FIND OUT WHY VERY SOON...

Blow jobs are trending in high schools. Oral sex is viewed as though it is not a big deal, research shows that young people don't really consider oral sex to be 'real sex'. It is very common to hear the stories of it happening in school bathrooms, behind bleachers, in the elevators, science labs, and at parties. We get the point — oral sex has become an epidemic in public places.

Oral sex (mouth to genitals. E.g. blow jobs, going down on someone, giving head) is a personal and intimate act that can be very enjoyable. However, it is degrading if we are doing it to fit in or to get someone to like us. People who do it casually at school might give an impression that 'it's whatever', but we've learned that sex involves our whole being. What does being so casual about such an intimate act do to our self-esteem or self-worth?

Petting (technical term for: sexually stimulating, caressing, and touching a partner). Heavy petting is great for foreplay (this is what you do to get your body ready for sex). So, if you want to wait to have sex-stay away from touching (or petting) erogenous zones (male genitals, female genitals, breast, neck) -

sensitive areas that can be highly sexually aroused.
Mutual masturbation (fingering, hand jobs). Many people enjoy doing and receiving this from a partner. It is common for people to do this before they have intercourse. Long make out sessions with a bit of heavy touching and then bam - you've gone all the way.

People who want to hold off on having sex before marriage are doing these things because they do not perceive these acts as being "real sex". Maybe you're thinking, like I used to think, that all of this non 'real sex' is fine because it's not actually "going all the way" (like intercourse). But why do we consider the act of intercourse as "going all the way"? Why is any one act better or more important than another when any behaviour that results in arousal, stimulation and gratification is sex? All sex is 'real sex'.

Fooling around is fun, we can't deny that. The idea of holding off on all this physical stuff is laughable to some, but hey - at the root of this discipline that is being asked of us, is that we would build healthy, strong, honest, trustworthy relationships with a person.

BLOW JOBS / HAND JOBS ETC.

DATING 101

1. TIMING IS CRUCIAL

Will the relationship get in the way of school or other commitments?

2. BEING INTENTIONAL IS NECESSARY.

3. WONDERING WHAT THE BIBLE SAYS?

There isn't much dating in the Bible — Most marriages were arranged!
Honor your parents- are they cool with you dating?
Jesus shows us relationships are about love and sacrifice- its all about putting the other first.

4. WHOSE RELATIONSHIP DO YOU LOOK UP TO AND WHY?

CHARACTERISTICS OF A HEALTHY RELATIONSHIP

1.   Sharing the same goals and values.
2.   Respect each other's boundaries.
3.   The timing is right.
4.   You pray about the relationship.
5.   Both prepared to work at making the relationship work.
6.   Parents and friends are supportive.
7.   Can you think of any others?

ARE YOU READY TO JOIN THE LOVE CLUB?

(Circle your answer)

1. WHEN YOU THINK ABOUT WHO YOU ARE AS A PERSON, IS YOUR DEFAULT THOUGHT:

a. That you like yourself and think your worthy of friendships and love.

b. About all the things you need to improve for someone else to like you.

2. BOUNDARIES ARE:

a. Good for a relationship.

b. Bad for a relationship.

3. REJECTION CAN HURT FROM THE ONE YOU LIKE   BECAUSE:

a. I "need" them to feel I have any kind of worth and value.

b. They compliment the worth and value that I already had.

4. WHICH OF THESE DETERMINES WHO IS A GOOD PERSON TO DATE?

a. Character, goals, sense of humor.

b. Popularity, looks, their smile.

*ANSWERS ON NEXT PAGE

1. CORRECT ANSWER: A (HEALTHY SELF-ESTEEM)

A healthy self-esteem affects your whole life - it determines how make choices, how you treat yourself and others, and how you allow others to treat you.

CHARACTERISTICS OF HEALTHY/UNHEALTHY SELF-ESTEEM

Feel good about yourself, self-respect / *Feel like you're not good enough.*
Positive, optimistic, hopeful / *Negative attitude about life.*
Are okay with life's challenges, don't expect to be perfect / *Reluctant to face fears.*
Don't depend on other's opinions / *Need approval from others.*
Are conformable with their boundaries and respect other's boundaries
Are okay with being assertive / *Feel detached and isolated from others.*
Inner-peace / *Difficulty connecting with inner-self.*

2. CORRECT ANSWER: A (ABILITY TO SET BOUNDARIES)

Boundaries are necessary to live out your values well. It's good to be upfront and on the same page about them.

BOUNDARIES TO CONSIDER

EMOTIONAL:
The 'L' word- if you're not ready to say it you don't have to!
Time apart is healthy, both people should be able to hang with friends and family and do things on their own if they like.

PHYSICAL:
Talk about it before the heat of the moment.
Take your time, don't rush into things.
Sex isn't a currency - you shouldn't have to do it to keep the relationship - you don't owe it to anyone!

DIGITAL:
What is okay and not okay to post on Facebook, Instagram, snapchat, etc.
Passwords: you shouldn't have to share - you are entitled to privacy.
Photo's and sexting: Once you send something, there is no taking it back and there are legal consequences.

3. CORRECT ANSWER: B (RESILIENCE TO ACCEPT REJECTION OR GRACEFULLY REJECT OTHERS)

It can be hard when someone calls it quits or when you have to. But dating is about figuring out what you like and don't like in a partner. You need to be able to call it quits if you don't think it's working.

EASIER SAID THAN DONE, HEY?

Tell your friends and family about your decision, they will help you stick to it.

Sometimes you still miss someone after a break up - you probably spent a lot of time with that person and shared special memories - that doesn't mean you're meant to be together, it just takes time.

4. CORRECT ANSWER: A (ABILITY TO CHOOSE THE RIGHT PERSON TO DATE)

The ability to choose the right person to date isn't saying it HAS to work out and you'll have to marry that person. Instead it's about understanding your own intentions and theirs. It takes some critical thinking.

LOOK FOR SOMEONE WHO:

HAS THE SAME VALUES AS YOU
RESPECTS YOU
LISTENS TO YOU
DOESN'T MAKE FUN OF YOU OR PUT YOU DOWN
IS PROUD OF YOUR ACCOMPLISHMENTS
CARING
HONEST
RESPECTS YOUR BOUNDARIES
UNDERSTAND THE IMPORTANCE OF HEALTHY RELATIONSHIPS
DOESN'T PRESSURE YOU.

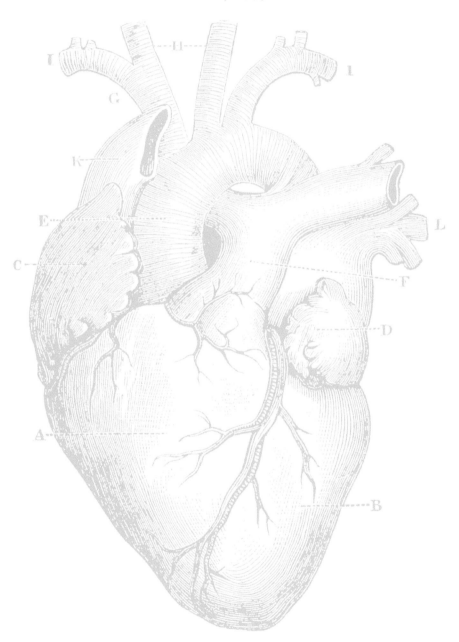

Fig. 37.

HEARTBREAK SUCKS.

As someone who has been there before and truly cares about every person reading this — I promise it'll be okay. You'll start to think about that person less and less day by day and then you will wake up one day, take a deep breath and will realize you moved on.
Heartbreak is for real - it hurts.

My two cents on getting over that person:
1.   You can always learn something from a bad situation. What did the relationship teach you about yourself? And what you would like in a future BF/GF?

2.   Embrace the pain - don't ignore how you feel; it's the key to wholeness. How did you feel about the breakup? Why?

3.   Your worth isn't determined on your relationship status; just because it didn't work out with a particular person doesn't mean you suck. Find or think of three things you love about yourself.

4.   Forgive, un-forgiveness and bitterness makes a toxic heart.

5.   God closes doors to protect. Oh it sucks at the time, but it just means something better is down the road.

6.   It gives you compassion for others facing the situation - you learn to be a good listener and a friend to someone.

Give God the benefit of the doubt, He literally cares about every area of our lives - (I know that from experience and well, the Bible says it) He definitely cares about who we date. If it didn't work out, He has a better plan for both involved, you don't have to have 'bad blood'; sometimes it just doesn't work out.

TELL ME A STORY OF YOUR DREAM RELATIONSHIP...

[your direct relationship story here]

SAME-SEX ATTRACTED AND CHRISTIAN

I think I'm gay (or same sex attracted), can I still be a christian?

I used to think no. I remember being a teenager and realising I was attracted to other guys and thinking there was something wrong with me. I would listen out for glimpses of same sex attraction being spoken of in church and the fragments I picked up had me conclude that people wouldn't want me in their lives if they found out. There were times I even feared I couldn't be saved if my sexuality didn't change.

Of course this wasn't true, but how would I know if no one ever talked about it?

I remember for about 6 years from the age of 14 almost every night in my room being on my knees sobbing before God and praying that He would change me, or 'heal' my orientation. It didn't shift.

When I was in my early twenties I had an incredible mentor who I fully opened up to. We met up every Tuesday for an hour for 2 years. She would listen radically, show grace and point me to the loving acceptance of God. It was largely through the consistency of these conversations that I came to a place of self-acceptance.

One night I remember deciding I was not going to pray, "God, please change me" anymore; instead I was going to pray, "God, please use me as I am." This prayer led to freedom.

I began to understand my sexuality didn't need to change for me to live a life wholly for God. And even if people chose not to accept me because of this I knew that, more importantly, **God accepted me and I could accept myself.**

To me it always seemed there were two options for an individual attracted to the same sex that is a Christian: option a) keep it inside, don't tell anyone and hope no one finds out, hope that it might change; option b) come out, tell people you're gay but leave the church, live a completely different lifestyle outside of Christian community.

I've decided there's got to be a new option. One that says "I'm a committed Christian and I'm attracted to the same sex (or gay, lesbian, bi), I'm not expecting my orientation to 'change', I completely accept myself, my sexuality is not my identity but I'm not denying it's a part of me, and I choose to live for God, build his kingdom and stay planted in my church community."

If I could offer advice from experience for anyone this relates to: you don't have to speak to everyone but it can be hugely healthy to talk to a friend, family member or mentor whom you know and trust.

And more than anything, know that you are loved just as you are.

— Danny

PORN

IS ARTIFICIAL SEXUAL STIMULATION.

ARTIFICIAL:
a copy of something that is meant to happen naturally.

STIMULATION:
raised levels of physiological or nervous activity in (the body or any biological system).

Why would we replace something that is meant to bring us REAL pleasure for something on a screen?

It's not just a moral, ethical or feminist argument anymore; numerous studies show the negative effect porn has on your brain. Science and psychology shows us how it is affecting individuals and relationships.

SEX is everywhere and soft porn is now the norm in our media (what was porn in the '60s is MTV in the 21st century)

Guys watch it. Girls watch it. Your friends may watch it. You may watch it. One time, occasionally, or on the reg. And did you know that today, the average age of someone viewing porn is 11?! Porn has become so easily accessible, that forming an addiction to it is just as easy.

Porn actually rewires your brain, whether you're addicted or not - watching it influences the way you think! And in turn can negatively affect your sex life.

It's hard to 'unlearn' things, (especially in our subconscious), and porn will mould a person's beliefs regarding sexuality and gender. For example, porn objectifies men and women (even if it is their free will to be in porn). It tells viewers that people are just objects to satisfy their desire, and can influence how you treat others both during sex and in everyday life.

First, let's look at some lies porn tells us about sex.

1. It's just you and the screen. It goes beyond the bedroom, The Journal of Adolescent Health states the effects of prolonged exposure to porn is - an exaggerated perception of sex in society; diminished trust between intimate couples; the abandonment of hope of sexual monogamy and the belief promiscuity is a natural state.

2. This is how 'to do' sex. Take a minute to think this through; if you're going to porn to teach you how to do sex, then that is what you EXPECT! So when you're in a real situation and it's not like you've expected, you're let down- you've put unrealistic pressure on your partner and you're less likely to be satisfied.

3. Porn stars do porn because they love sex. Yes, a lot of porn stars choose to be in porn, but not just because they love sex, it's a means to an end to pay bills! A big issue is, young girls are being capitalized (taken advantage of, profit from, exploited) for just their bodies. It's all about the money; porn producers are taking advantage of vulnerable and impressionable young girls (manipulating their insecurities) and promising quick money and fame. Once you're in, it's hard to get out.

4. Its real. Its a false reality, ha yeah right!! Girls are just SO happy to be thrown around and just there to please the man, sorry guys - girls want, need, and deserve pleasure too. (Sex is about both GIVING and receiving pleasure). There are awkward noises in sex, girls take like 45 minutes to be aroused, in porn - they are just ready right then. "Porn is not a problem 'cause it shows too much, but it shows too little". - Unknown

5. It's embracing that it's
natural to be sexual. Being sexual
is GOOD and natural, but sexual
exploitation cannot be justified
as "its just sexual". Porn is not
embracing healthy sexuality - it is
objectifying women. It belittles
women to merely the object of men's
sexual desire. A great friend of
mine explains it like this, "You
abandon yourself to a mindless lust
that ignores your ethics, aesthetic
taste and relational morality" (Aimee
Gardine)

You feel like you get all this, but
just don't actually know how to stop…
next up, there are some action steps.

Sex addiction and porn addiction
(different from each other) is real
thing.

HOW TO KNOW IF YOU'RE ADDICTED:
Compulsion to use / Continued use
in spite of adverse consequences /
Inability to Control use / Craving -
psychological or physical.

HOW IT WORKS:
The reward center (nucleus accumbens)
doesn't know what porn is[6]. It only
registers levels of stimulation
through dopamine spikes. This is
physiology, not morality or sexual
politics.

ADDICTION 101:
Desensitization: Makes you less
sensitive to what would normally
give you pleasure and 'hungry' for
more. Creates a need for more intense
stimulation.

Sensitization: There is a tug of war
in your brain between the craving
pathways and your executive control.

TIPS TO BEAT ADDICTION:

1. Delete stash

2. Destroy all physical porn (DVDs, magazines)

3. Install an Internet porn blocker and put it on the strictest settings. Put in a
password that you don't have memorized, write it down and put it in a difficult
place to retrieve. Check out XXXchurch.com

4. Try to limit computer time, and if you experience a trigger or a serious urge,
then shut off your computer and do a pre-set activity that will now be your "go-to" porn replacement activity. Choose something positive and healthy: chess, exercise, eat a salad, study a language etc.

5. Stop masturbating for as long as you can stand. If you must masturbate, then do it without porn.

6. Continually update your journal with your experiences and insights.

7. If you do use porn again, don't give up.

8. Do whatever it takes to stay away from porn and do quit masturbating for as long as possible.

9. Resist the urge to "test" yourself with porn. That can send you right back into it.

10. DO NOT!!! LISTEN TO YOUR BRAIN! If you're gonna reboot, then do it and ignore all rationalizations. After two months or so, you can think whatever you want as far as "Does it really work?" or "Should I continue?"

PORN IS ARTIFICIAL SEXUAL STIMULATION.

(Taken from yourbrainonporn.com)

[END OF MAGAZINE]

[END OF MAGAZINE]

+ ENDNOTES

How to read this book:
Keller, Tim. *"The Gospel and Sex."* Web log post. Qideas.org. N.p., 2005. Web.

Week 1
[1] Genesis 1:31 *God looked over everything he had made; it was so good, so very good! It was evening, it was morning— Day Six.*
[2] Weerakoon, Patricia, Dr. *"What Is Sex and What Does God Think about It."* Teen Sex by the Book. Sydney South, N.S.W.: Anglican Youthworks, 2013. 24. Print.
[3] Keller, Tim. *"The Gospel and Sex."* Web log post. Qideas.org. N.p., 2005. Web.
[4] Elwell, Walter A. *"Baker's Evangelical Dictionary of Biblical Theology-Marriage."* Bible Study Tools. Baker Books, 1996. Web. 24 May 2014.
[5] Fisher, Helen E., Phd, Arthur Aron, Phd, Debra Mashek, MA, Haifang Li, Phd, and Lucy L. Brown, Phd. *"Defining the Brain Systems of Lust, Romantic Attraction, and Attachment."* Archives of Sexual Behaviour 31.5 (2002): 413-19. Print.
[6] Siegel, Daniel J. *"Attachment How Relationships and the Brain Interact to Shape Who We Are."* The Developing Mind: Toward a Neurobiology of Interpersonal Experience. New York: Guilford, 1999. 66-120. Print.

Week 2
[1] Heinrichs, Markus, Bernadette Von Dawans, and Gregor Domes. *"Oxytocin, Vasopressin, and Human Social Behaviour."* Frontiers in Neuroendocrinology 30.4 (2009): 548-57. Web.
[2] Fisher, H. E., A. Aron, and L. L. Brown. *"Romantic Love: A Mammalian Brain System for Mate Choice."* Philosophical Transactions of the Royal Society B: Biological Sciences 361.1476 (2006): 2173-186. Web
[3] Casey, B., N. Tottenham, C. Liston, and S. Durston. *"Imaging the Developing Brain: What Have We Learned about Cognitive Development?"* Trends in Cognitive Sciences 9.3 (2005): 104-10. Web.
[4] Young, Larry J. *"Being Human: Love: Neuroscience Reveals All."* Nature 457.7226 (2009): 148. Web

Week 3
[1] U.S. Department of Health and Human Services. *"Developing Adolescents."* APA: American Psychological Association . Accessed February 24, 2014, http://www.apa.org/pi/families/resources/develop.pdf.
[2] The Century of the Self. Perf. Adam Curtis. BBC, 2001. Television Documentary.
[3] Luke 15: 1-7 *By this time a lot of men and women of doubtful reputation were hanging around Jesus, listening intently. The Pharisees and religion scholars were not pleased, not at all pleased. They growled, "He takes in sinners and eats meals with them, treating them like old friends." Their grumbling triggered this story. "Suppose one of you had a hundred sheep and lost one. Wouldn't you leave the ninety-nine in the wilderness and go after the lost one until you found it? When found, you can be sure you would put it across your shoulders, rejoicing, and when you got home call in your friends and neighbors, saying, 'Celebrate with me! I've found my lost sheep!' Count on it—there's more joy in heaven over one sinner's rescued life than over ninety-nine good people in no need of rescue.*

[4] "Violence against Women- Intimate Partner and Sexual Violence against Women." Http://www.who.int/mediacentre/factsheets/fs239/en/. N.p., Nov. 2014. Web.

Week 4
[1] Dictionary.com
[2] Fisher, Helen E., Phd, Arthur Aron, Phd, Debra Mashek, MA, Haifang Li, Phd, and Lucy L. Brown, Phd. *"Defining the Brain Systems of Lust, Romantic Attraction, and Attachment."* Archives of Sexual Behaviour 31.5 (2002): 413-19. Print.3
[3] http://www.advocatesforyouth.org [cited:07.07.2016]
[4] Peck, M. Scott. *"The Road Less Traveled: A New Psychology of Love, Traditional Values, and Spiritual Growth."* New York: Simon and Schuster, 1978. Print
[5] https://en.wikipedia.org/wiki/Desire
[6] Mere Christianity by C.S. Lewis

Week 5
[1] Proverbs 10:17 *The road to life is a disciplined life; ignore correction and you're lost for good.*
[2] *"The Happiness Trap: Stop Struggling, Start Living"* by Russ Harris
[3] Galatians 5:13-15 *It is absolutely clear that God has called you to a free life. Just make sure that you don't use this freedom as an excuse to do whatever you want to do and destroy your freedom. Rather, use your freedom to serve one another in love; that's how freedom grows. For everything we know about God's Word is summed up in a single sentence: Love others as you love yourself. That's an act of true freedom. If you bite and ravage each other, watch out—in no time at all you will be annihilating each other, and where will your precious freedom be then?*

Magazine
[1] Romans 7:5; 8:6, 13
[2] urbandictionary.com
[3] https://www.youtube.com/watch?v=Tad9Q9OFjJw
[4] Veale, David, Sarah Miles, Sally Bramley, Gordon Muir, and John Hodsoll. *"Am I Normal? A Systematic Review and Construction of Nomograms for Flaccid and Erect Penis Length and Circumference in up to 15 521 Men."* BJU International BJU Int 115.6 (2015): 978-86. Web. 4 Mar. 2015.
[5] Mitchell, Anne, Kent Patrick, Wendy Heywood, Pamela Blackman, and Marian Pitts. 5th National Survey of Australian Secondary Students and Sexual Health 2013. N.p.: n.p., n.d. Print.
[6] *"Start Here for a Brief Overview of Concepts and Science."* Start Here for a Brief Overview of Concepts and Science. N.p., n.d. Web. 14 Sept. 2014.

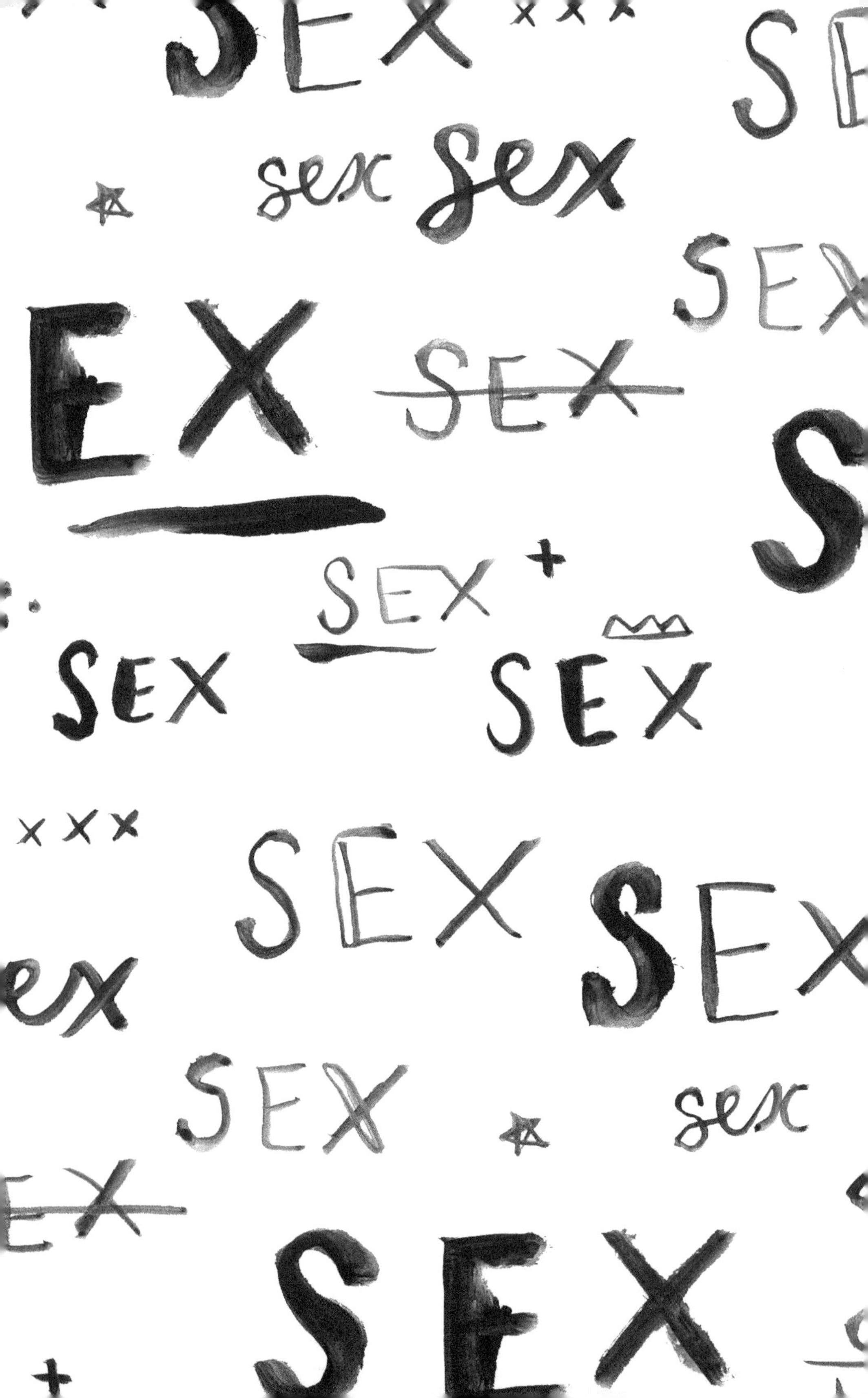

sex
Sex
SEX
SEX
SEX
SEX
SEX
SEX
SEX
SEX
sex
SEX

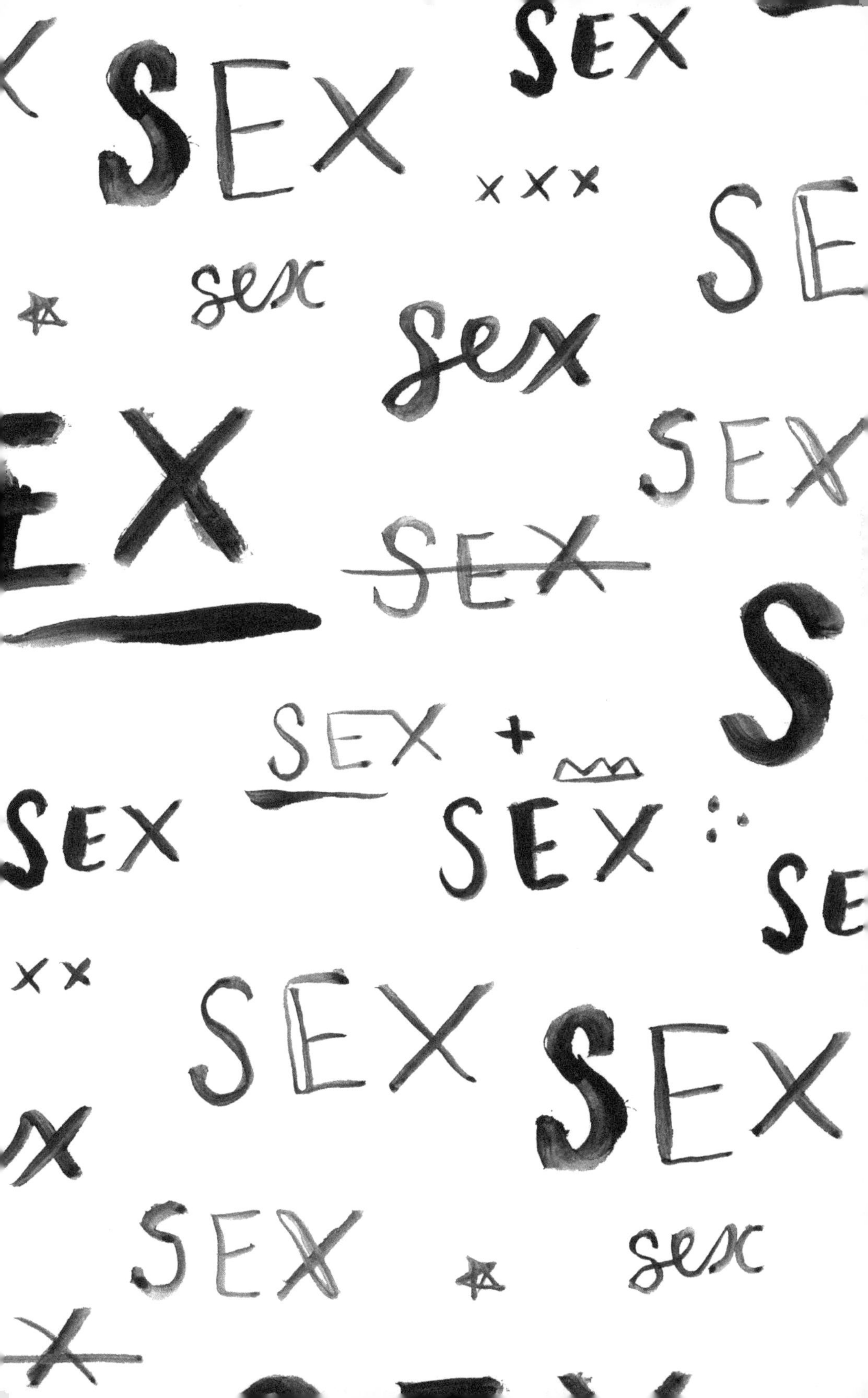
SEX
SEX
sex
sex
SEX
SEX
SEX
SEX
SEX
SEX
SEX
SEX
sex

CPSIA information can be obtained
at www.ICGtesting.com
Printed in the USA
BVHW02s1919020318
509565BV00006B/6/P